For the still

Sick and suffering

The Funny Thing About Being Sober

By John C. Wolfe

You Can't Die: A Day of Clarity (2016), The Funny Thing About Being Sober (2018)

Contents

Preface..........................5

1. Nightmare on Fremont Street............6
2. The Chowder Still Flies on Christmas............25
3. Da Nile is More Than a River........................31
4. Sushi Over Strawberries..........................54
5. Death is Funny...................................61
6. The 90s Are Over...............................67
7. And This is My Brain on Pizza...................96
8. Juan and the Killer Turkeys...........................110
9. Andy From Above....................................120
10. The Tangled Relationships of AA...................131
11. The Only Requirement for What?...................141
12. The Wrath of Grapes...........................157
13. George's Curiosity............................167
14. When Life Gives You Lemons...........................176
15. The Gross Glory of Reaching Out 192
16. The Politics of Not Drinking...........................214
17. Cars Don't Make People Crazy, People Make People Crazy.......230
18. If You Build It, They Are Dumb........................241
19. Boon's Day in the Day..............................255
20. A Funny Thing Happened on the Way Back to Detox....……..259
21. OMG, Did You Hear What Joe Said About Frank?............269
22. A Bridge to Narcan........................…..273
23. My Viral Disease....................…..280
24. Jackson's Hell..................290
25. Didn't God Make Lamotrigine?...............298

Afterword...........308
About the Author   311
Amazon and Kindle Reviews 313

"Proving you're not crazy
is like proving you're not racist.
The harder you try, the worse you sound."

~You Can't Die: A Day of Clarity

John C. Wolfe

Preface

I DIDN'T PLAN ON WRITING a sequel to *You Can't Die: A Day of Clarity*. I didn't think it would be necessary or, for that matter, interesting. The reviews for the first book were outstanding and flattering. Of the forty-nine reviews on Amazon and Kindle, forty-eight gave the book five-stars, and one gave it four.

But a few of the reviewers were wondering what happened after I finally got sober:

> *"...This novel by Mr. Wolfe didn't just spark with me, it lit a whole fire. Well written, sir. The only criticism I have -- and this is minor -- I wanted to know more, like how he's maintaining his sobriety now, how have his friendships and family dynamics evolved, etc. But then again, you always leave your audience wanting more."* **~Amazon Review, B.A. Baker**

Honestly, I thought that once I ran out of outrageous drinking and fighting stories to tell, the book would get boring, so I gave the first book a brief happy ending and typed "The End."

You Can't Die: A Day of Clarity is a story about a human catastrophe. That's what makes it interesting. A lot of people who read the book -- some who know me, but most who don't – disagree. They think the four years after I got sober have been far more entertaining to watch, mostly on social media. My behavior certainly gets more of the right kind of attention these days. By that, I mean it gets the attention of family and friends and social media and the occasional newspaper or TV station. But, *is* it the right kind of attention? You decide. To me, it doesn't matter. I'm just being myself, entertaining my family and staying sober – one ridiculous day at a time.

Chapter One

Nightmare on Fremont Street

THREE WEEKS SOBER

The two drunk guys sitting next to me wanted to "do" my wife, and just because she wasn't officially my wife yet, I still felt like I should at least give someone a look of disapproval.

Then again, it's not like she was in the local library reading "The Canterbury Tales." She was on a stage in a bikini and high heels -- in Las Vegas, in front of a thousand people.

I was sitting in the audience, sweating and anxious, about twenty rows back next to Dumb and Dumber, listening as they rated her ass. And although the reviews were overwhelmingly good, this is not where I was supposed to be three weeks after rehab.

On the plane the day before, my nose was pressed to the window as we passed over the Rockies. All I could think about was the lake house, which had remained abandoned since my Mom and aunt spooned my drunken, near-death body out of there two months earlier.

But here I was flying over the breathtaking Rocky Mountains with my equally-breathtaking fiancé en route to Las Vegas. What man wouldn't be grateful to be doing all this with a woman who held his hand through countless drunken missteps, rehabs and hospitals?

We were just beginning our descent to Vegas, I was looking for the Grand Canyon – the one I should have been looking for 200 miles ago – when Lisa spoke for the first time in over an hour.

"Talk to me honey. I'm starting to get really anxious about this competition."

High maintenance bitch. At first, I thought that'd be a funny thing to say, but then I saw that she was clearly in a bad place.

"You'll be a winner as soon as you step on the stage," I told her. "There's no one here to prove anything to. It's just you and me and a bunch of total strangers."

It was tough to spit all of that out when I didn't want her to do the show at all. I would rather have said, "You're right, fuck it. Let's get drunk and hit the tables."

The night before the competition, Lisa was justifiably concerned about how I was going to spend my time alone while she was backstage for most of the day.

"Are you going to be okay?"

"Why wouldn't I be?"

Maybe it was the sea of booze or the gambling. Or maybe she worried that her fiancé, still drooling from his last rehab, shouldn't be surrounded by cocktail waitresses dressed like hookers passing out free beer.

"I'll be fine," I kept telling her.

But clearly, I wasn't where I was supposed to be, at least not according to my rehab counselors and the folks at AA. They told me the same thing a hundred times: During your first year of sobriety, don't make any major decisions (like getting engaged). Don't do anything unusual (like flying from rehab to Vegas). And avoid people (like alcoholics), places (like casinos) and things (like 24-hour bars) that could be a trigger to drink.

There's a reason they want you to avoid big decisions. When you're suddenly sober after drinking alcoholically for twenty-five years, the world is a big foggy puzzle. Everything is confusing and unfamiliar. I wasn't just confused; I was delusional, one step away from hearing voices. I needed constant instruction and was constantly asking Lisa, "What do I do now?"

The simplest decisions left me paralyzed with fear and uncertainty. I'd come to a stop sign and stay there, looking left, looking right, looking behind me.

There wouldn't be another car in sight, but I'd just sit there, waiting until it seemed like there wasn't a chance in hell I could hit anything. The squirrels in our neighborhood turned me into a basket case... the way they run into the middle of the road, stop and stare, then run back where they came from, and do the whole thing over again. I love all animals, but squirrels can be assholes.

I didn't trust myself; I needed someone else to tell me what to do. If there was no one around to do that, I either did something stupid or did nothing.

I had two GPS's, one on a smart phone that I bought after the Vegas trip and one in my car. I didn't know about the one on my phone and I couldn't figure out how to power on the one in the car. Finally, I asked Lisa for help and she showed me how to plug it in.

I hate to cite something so objectionable to make the point, but I remember feeling like Gary Busey in the Amazon Fire TV Stick TV Commercials. Busey, a great actor in his day, suffered brain damage in a motorcycle accident.

In the Amazon commercial, he comes off as severely retarded while trying to plug a seashell into a USB port.

I remember seeing that commercial for the first time and feeling sorry for him, which, of course, meant I was feeling sorry for myself.

Today, four years out of rehab, it's much different... kind of. People are constantly telling me I act like a five-year-old – and I do. But when I first got out of rehab, I *felt* like a five-year-old -- a lost five-year-old -- and Las Vegas is a bad place for a lost five-year-old, especially if he's an alcoholic.

The competition was taking place at the renowned Golden Nugget on Fremont Street so Lisa booked our room there just to make everything easy. But the Golden Nugget is anything but easy. It's a giant house of mirrors, its own, vice-ridden town with a thousand acres of casinos, four towers and ten thousand guys with hairy chests, gold chains and bad manners.

Two of the towers are called the North Tower and the South Tower. Apparently, the Gold Nugget didn't get the memo on September 12, 2001.

I was looking around, disoriented, nervous, confused and sweating. I couldn't figure out how to use my cell phone. I forgot how to spell four syllable words, like "oblivious." I could barely construct simple sentences like, "John was supposed to go to AA meetings but instead he went to Las Vegas and got drunk."

I lost all sense of direction. I couldn't find my way anywhere. On foot, I darted around like a mouse on Ritalin. In the car... honestly, they should have shredded my license.

If a cop had pulled me over, he would have run me through all the tests – standing on one foot, eyes to nose, alphabet backwards – all of it. He'd have breathalyzed me, taken urine, drawn blood, done a tox screen... and when he was all done, and I'd passed every single test, he would have arrested my jittery ass anyway.

It's hilarious now, but when it was happening, I was depressed -- thoroughly ashamed of what I'd become. I had euphoric highs with bursts of energy, but they were sporadic and brief. They'd disappear as soon as they came, and then I'd go back to being dumb and depressed.

I kept telling myself that, as miserable as I was when they shoveled my drunk and dying ass out of the lake house, I was still happier than I was sober and incompetent. That's not a healthy thought for an alcoholic to have in early recovery, especially when he's stumbling around Las Vegas.

In person, you could tell I was sober. On social media, I was barely articulate, and I guarantee a lot of my old friends thought I was drinking again – although, my former colleagues from the

Governor's Office must have realized that, if that were the case, I would sound brilliant.

THE GOLDEN NUGGET is a glitzy world with gold elevator doors, mirrored hallways with glittering chandeliers. Lisa had several appointments the day before the competition. She was having her hair done at one of the towers that afternoon. Here's how that went:

We walked out of our room and down the hall to the elevators which we took down to the lobby. Then we walked down a long glitzy hallway to another lobby, then walked outside about a hundred yards to the tower we were looking for. We took the elevator up to the whatever-th floor and walked down a long hall to room number whatever.

At that point, my life was in Lisa's hands because if we got separated and I needed to get back to the room, I would call 911.

Then comes the Mother-of-All luxury problems. We walked into the small room where a few very attractive, scantily-clad girls were getting their hair done.

They were all very nice to me, but I was the only guy in the room and it felt awkward, especially because the only place for me to hang out was on the bed.

One or two of the women made small talk with me. Every time they asked me a question, I stuttered something back while scraping sweat off my forehead with the room key card.

I bet the average guy would pay a lot of money to be in that room, but not nearly as much as I would have paid to be back at our own room watching Sesame Street and sucking my thumb.

Then terror struck.

Lisa forgot something back at our Tower, whatever the name of it was, and the woman doing her hair was telling her how important it was that she have it right then and there.

"We can get it later, right," I said.

"I don't think we'll have time, honey. Do you mind?"

"Uh...."

"What's wrong?" she asked.

Fuck! There was no place to pull her aside for a private conversation. I wasn't going to admit I couldn't find my way back to the room in front of all those swimsuit models.

"Nothing is wrong. I'm going back there right now to get that... thing. What does it look like?"

But I couldn't even get that part right. It was a... a thing, a yellow thing you wear around your whatever.

"What's our room number again?"

She told me the room number as I was walking out the door. As soon as the door shut behind me, I forgot what it was.

I made it to the elevator, and I knew I was going to take it down.

From there, I was screwed. Even if I found my way to the room, I'd never figure out how to get back to Tower Wherever, not without a compass and a bucket of breadcrumbs.

Any solution requiring a cell phone wasn't an option because I didn't know how to use a smartphone yet, and I didn't have one anyway.

I didn't want to look dumb or drunk by walking in circles, so I sat down in the lobby, looking around for clues about where to go next.

I was worried I wouldn't be able to find Lisa's yellow thing, so I took a few minutes to feel sorry for myself. Guys were walking around with beer bottles, laughing.

Stay focused. Find the room.

I wasn't sure if I was heading in the right direction but started walking faster anyway since time was a factor. I'll skip the tedious details, but I came to a set of elevators, and made it to the right floor... but I was in the wrong tower. They were all gold, so...

The smartest thing I did all day was asking for help. The woman at the front desk scanned my room key card and gave me directions to my room. She helped me reconstruct my way back to the room with all the women in it, and she was even kind enough to write a few things down for me.

"Thanks for writing it down," I told her. "It's for my wife. She gets turned around so easily."

It was a silly lie, since I was the one who asked for help.

I still don't know what the yellow thing was, but it was the only yellow thing in Lisa's suitcase and I found it, then followed the directions back to the other room. It was a twenty-minute errand that took just over an hour.

I walked in the room and one of the women said, "There he is!"

Lisa let out a big sigh of relief.

I knew she was going to ask what took so long. The one thing I was getting good at in early sobriety is deflecting questions like that by just throwing out random words.

"Is everything okay, honey? You were gone a long time."

"Yeah, they were just having the thing fixed, and the doors back at the other tower had to be unlocked so the guy told me it was going to take a while."

"Oh, okay."

FIVE O'CLOCK IS a stupid time to wake up but, the next day, Lisa did it anyway. She had to be at the theater early and was already gone by the time I woke up an hour later.

The competition was supposed to start around noon, but I began walking over there at eight o'clock because, the way things were going, I could easily wind up in Reno.

Four casinos separated our room from the theater, so there was no way to get there without smelling alcohol every step of the way.

There might have been a way to get there by walking outside, but my big, colorful idiot map showed a simple straight line, and I wasn't straying from it.

People were already drinking, and it was only eight-thirty in the morning, which disgusted me until I remembered that I used to start at seven.

In one casino after the other, people were working the tables, drinking and pulling levers. I was thinking about Lisa's contest. I was severely anxious about it for a hundred different reasons, most of which I couldn't explain.

As I got closer to the theater, I began to sweat, and my heart was racing. I felt like I was back on the Million Dollar Staircase in the State Capitol.

It felt like it was raining alcohol. There were young waitresses in lingerie uniforms everywhere, and they were all holding trays with glasses of beer. They were passing them out like hors d'oeuvres.

I remembered thinking how easily I could drink an entire tray without taking a breath. I also remember wanting to.

I stopped walking and stared at one of the trays. Way too much time went by before I realized I'd been staring too long, and the young woman holding the tray was staring back, sort of challenging my rudeness. Until then, I hadn't even noticed *her*.

I'm not staring at you, bitch. I want the beer.

I shook my head a little, like I was waking myself up after zoning out, just to let her know I wasn't sweating because of her.

For a couple of reasons, it was time to walk away. Problem was, everywhere I walked, there was another Hooters girl passing out free beer.

To be clear: By mentioning the pretty women in the same breath as the free beer, I'm not suggesting that I was tempted by both. The prettiest woman in Vegas that morning was the one in the theater waiting for her fiancé.

The second prettiest was the one carrying around the most beer. To an alcoholic fresh from rehab, Harvey Weinstein would look pretty holding a tray of beer.

I was not in a good place, and I was already formulating excuses and cover stories. I came dangerously close to convincing myself that getting lost would be a plausible excuse to drink, the logic being that a few drinks would clear me up, so I could get unlost.

The other thought I had – and I'm not proud to admit it -- was that I could simply blame Lisa for bringing me to Vegas.

Of course, this trip was planned before I went to the Caron Foundation. If I hadn't run away from the place, I would have seven months of sobriety under my belt by the time we got to Vegas.

None of the waitresses had offered me a beer yet, probably because I wasn't standing close enough to the slot machines. I was standing where people walk, not gamble.

Maybe I should sit in front of a slot machine, just to test myself.

I walked over to the slots and stood in front of one for a few seconds. Out of the corner of my eye, I could see one of the waitresses coming my way. My heart was racing.

Get the fuck out of here, now!

About an hour later, I was patting myself on the back for passing the test. I know now that I wasn't really testing myself; I was looking for an excuse to drink. Luckily, there wasn't one readily available... at least, not at that moment.

BUT NOW I WAS IN THE THEATER, being tested once more, this time by Dumb and Dumber. With these two rutting morons pushing my buttons, excuses were flying at me from every direction as they sized up Lisa's ass, legs and breasts.

"That's a good one," said Dumb.

"Yeah," said Dumber.

"Oh yeah."

"Yeah, right there."

"Yeah."

It sounded like they were jerking each other off.

A year ago, the punches would have been flying after the first "Yeah."

But now, still groggy from the rehab, I knew I had to at least try some of the coping suggestions they'd given me there. Did I say the serenity prayer? Hell no. But I didn't turn the auditorium into a crime scene either.

In fact, at first, I didn't react at all. I simply clapped and cheered hard for my wife, hoping Dumb and Dumber would get the message. They kinda did, and I was thanking God for that because my days of fighting more than one guy at a time were over. I wasn't mad enough anymore.

17

As soon as Lisa exited the stage, I left the auditorium, hoping to see her in the lobby before her next appearance on stage.

The day was a test for both of us. For the first time in her life, Lisa, who has always been fanatical about her physique, was competing in a fitness contest – on a stage -- in a bikini – in Las Vegas – with over a thousand people watching her.

That day, we both needed more support and attention than the other could provide. For about twelve hours, we were being in a city that truly is sinful if you're not prepared for it.

No one was watching me in the casino, but it's ludicrous to think I could have gotten away with a couple drinks to "calm my nerves." I am physically and mentally incapable of stopping at one drink, or even fifteen. I would have continued to drink until I passed out.

Whatever happened in Vegas wouldn't have stayed in Vegas because the final shock to my system would have killed me.

In other words, the nasty look I got from the French Maid with the tray of beer probably saved my life. I'll let someone else break the news to her. It's bound to make her day.

Lisa and I went to dinner that night at a Steak House once frequented by Frank, Sammy and Dean. For Millennials, that's Sinatra, Davis and Martin.

I was shaking a lot at the table. I didn't want to embarrass myself by trying to get a soup spoon to my mouth, so I let it cool off and drank it from the bowl. Lisa started laughing her ass off.

"Oh, shut up and cut my steak," I told her.

This isn't how I thought life after drinking would be. For twenty-five years, my mom fought for this. I owe her my life, but I wasn't yet convinced that living like this was worth it. I wasn't miserable enough to kill myself – not even close -- but I could easily get miserable enough to drink again, which is the same thing.

Now, I had Lisa, and I know my mom was grateful for that. To this day, there's only person alive who knows why Lisa stayed with me through all the chaos, and that's Lisa.

But, hard as she tried, Lisa couldn't be by my side 24/7. She couldn't save me from myself, not in Las Vegas and not even while sitting right next to me at the Hokkaido Sushi Restaurant in New Paltz, New York.

That's where I inadvertently broke my sobriety.

LISA AND I WERE SEATED around the cooking table – it's called a teppanyaki table -- with three other couples. The chef – I'll call him Mr. Haiku, since the only other Japanese word I know is teppanyaki -- was juggling knives, flicking shrimp and starting our food on fire. In the middle of all that, Mr. Haiku pointed at my mouth.

"Open! Open!"

I opened it wide, thinking he was going to flick a little piece of chicken in my mouth.

Instead, he whipped out a big squirt container, pointed it in my mouth and squeezed, sending a stream of what felt and tasted like warm rubbing alcohol to the back of my throat. Yes, I know what rubbing alcohol tastes like.

It happened so fast. One second, I was sitting there admiring everyone else's Sapporo, the next second my two months of sobriety was circling the drain.

Lisa and I looked at each other in horror. I spit some of it into a napkin, but most of it went down my throat.

"What the fuck was that?" I yelled.

"It was Saki," she yelled back. "Did it go down?"

"Most of it did. I need to do something."

The other couples at the table knew something was up but I think most of them just figured I was just a pansy who couldn't handle Saki.

"How do you feel?" Lisa asked.

"It registered... I can feel it. I'll just drink a lot of water and concentrate on something else."

Mr. Haiku was pretty good with that squirter. He must have emptied at least one shot of Saki into my mouth. Even if only half of it made it into my system, that's the equivalent of half a beer, which is all it takes to initiate a relapse.

When an alcoholic's brain detects booze, even a little, it's like flipping a switch. Once that happens, it's over. You drink a gallon of water, but you can't unring the bell.

I got the impression that Lisa was leery about the whole thing. I forgot her exact words, but whatever she said seemed to imply that I could have reacted quicker.

With just one month out of rehab, I wasn't doing *anything* quick… well, one thing. Other than that, I needed a pep talk just to cook a pizza.

I was like a criminal surrounded by cops with their guns cocked. I wasn't making any sudden movements that could be perceived as irrational or threatening.

I was too timid and unsure to make simple decisions. I couldn't even decide whether I should be brushing my teeth up and down or side to side. I still don't know.

BUT I WOKE UP feeling brave one morning, brushed my teeth both ways and headed to Saratoga to buy a cell phone. That probably doesn't sound like much, but when you're segregated from technology for ten years, it's not easy to catch up with the rest of the world in fifteen minutes. That's how long a sales dude will spend teaching you things before getting impatient and snotty.

The last cell phone I owned had a big antenna and typewriter keys. I had been so isolated at the lake house, I'd never even seen a smart phone. The second I walked into the Verizon store, I looked around and felt like my IQ had been cut in half, right down to twenty-three.

I was determined to pull this thing off without Lisa's help.

They didn't have what I was looking for, which was a flip phone. All they had were things that, to me, looked like shiny black rectangles. Apparently, they were phones, but they didn't have buttons or antennas.

To me, they all looked identical, but the twenty-year-old hipster behind the counter gawked at me like I was a baboon when I asked him why. He decided to give me a crash course on phone features, like a waiter going over the lunch specials.

He was talking in a language I didn't understand, saying things like too-jee, three-jee and for-jee and geo-tag. He knew I didn't understand, so he spoke slow and bitchy-like.

I asked him how many free minutes I'd get for signing up.

"They're *all* free since like, *ever*."

"I need something basic," I told him.

He reached under the counter where they keep phones for Civil War veterans and showed me another shiny black rectangle.

"More basic than that. I want one with buttons on the front."

Now it seemed like he was getting annoyed.

"The *buttons*," he said, with a prickly emphasis on *buttons*, "are at the bottom."

Then he slid his finger across the bottom of the shiny black rectangle and spoke to me in a long drawn out voice. I swore he was trying to do it with a southern accent.

"See, the buttons are right here -- home button, back button and search button."

Oh, I get it – you want to fight.

I just stared at him for a few seconds, watching him nod slowly at me. I wanted to smash the fucking phone into his face.

Instead, I took a deep breath and composed myself.

"No, I mean the number buttons," I said. "One, two, three… you know, like when I wanna make a telephone call."

"All of them have numbers when you turn it on."

He was still using the southern accent on me. I needed to get out of there quick, before I pulled him over the counter.

"I have to go to the bathroom!"

I walked away as fast as I could and never went back.

If I had any hopes of staying sober, that's what I had to do – and I'd just done it for the second time since leaving rehab. I was pleased with myself.

The following week, after researching phones online, I walked into Best Buy like I owned the place. This time, I knew exactly what I was looking for. All I had to do is ask for it, give them a credit card and leave.

When I got to the area with all the shiny black rectangles called phones, I went straight to the counter.

"I need a Samsung Galaxy Three."

"Hmm, I don't know if we have any of those dinosaurs left. Why a Three and not a Four?"

"That's what I meant -- Four."

He reached under the counter and pulled out three of them.

Oh shit, here we go. He's gonna ask me something.

"What do you think – black, blue or white?" he asked.

That's easy. I got this.

"I'll go with white again."

And that was it. He needed a bunch of personal information, like my name, but Lisa wrote all that stuff down for me.

I must have picked a good phone because they charged me $700 dollars for it.

"Let's go over the features," the guy said.

Yeah, fuck that. I wasn't going to subject myself to that humiliation twice in one lifetime.

"I'll just read the owner's manual or operator's instructions," I told him. "Just show me how to turn it on one more time."

Chapter Two

The Chowder Still Flies

SEVEN WEEKS SOBER

The manager at the Olive Garden was uncomfortable. He looked like he'd rather be sitting on Harvey Weinstein's lap than standing in front of our table. We could tell he was about to give us a lecture, so we did our best to ensure he was twice as uncomfortable when he finished as he was when he started.

"So, I'm here to talk with the loud table," he said, as a spitball sailed past his left ear.

"We need more rolls," I yelled from the far end of the table.

There were ten of us, and we looked like an unlikely group to warrant the censure of a restaurant manager. A pair of grandparents, four parents and four kids – aka, my immediate and very seasoned family.

"We're just celebrating," my Mom said.

"I just got out of rehab," I yelled.

My brother looked back at the manager. "How are ya doing with those rolls?"

Our long table was set back from the main dining room with small partition walls separating us from everyone else. Maybe one of the million spitballs that started flying the moment we sat down made it past the partitions and pelted an innocent customer.

My 82nd Airborne brother brushed it off as "collateral damage."

The table talk that night was loud, raunchy and totally unacceptable in a restaurant. Admittedly, the worst of it was coming from me.

Being sober in a public setting like an Olive Garden was still an unusual thing for me. I'd only been sober for a few months, so I was a long way from walking out of the cloud. But I was with my fiancée and family and I was full of energy.

The spitballs started flying about four seconds after the host seated us, and they were made of everything from napkins to candle wax – anything that you could cram in a straw.

When the dinner rolls arrived, balls of bread started flying too.

The whole thing started when my brother sent a stinger into my son. By the time it was over, my Mom -- tired of being a pacifist and a target -- was firing back... with zero skill. She was so happy to see the whole family together -- healthy and having fun -- she'd have joined in no matter what we were doing.

At the opposite end of the table, Lisa wasn't sure what to do, whether to grab a straw or cancel the wedding. Mallory, who had just turned old enough to swear without getting punished, was dropping the F-bomb like an ex-con.

There was an armistice when the appetizers came, an armistice that lasted as long as it took my brother to inhale his pizzaiola flatbread. As was his wont, he rolled the flatbread up to the size of a rolling pin, guided it into his mouth, and like a sword swallower, slid the whole thing down his throat.

At some point, it must have unrolled itself. On an MRI, the flatbread would look like a manta ray swimming around in my brother's stomach. Once his hands were free, the armistice was over, as he reloaded and started firing again.

Now that bits of food were being used as live ammunition, my two pretty nieces tried guarding their hair with their jackets. I would think my brother's children would know better. The ones trying hardest not to get hit are always the primary targets.

Back at the north end of the table, a funny thought popped into my head – a thought that unquestionably validated my ticket to hell. It was so tasteless and insensitive, I never even considered printing it here. I didn't even want to say it out loud that night because I knew my twisted, like-minded daughter would spit her food out laughing if I did – and then I would get blamed for causing her to do it.

So, I whispered it in her ear instead.

I waited until she had a mouthful of food, hoping that, when it came flying out of her mouth, some or all of it would hit Jackson on the other side of the table. I was to show my family that their plan wasn't working, that sending me to rehab wouldn't make me any more civilized.

I leaned over and started to whisper in Mallory's ear, but couldn't compose myself long enough to say anything. That's when I decided it would be better to keep my twisted thoughts and ideas to myself. So, I sat back and returned to my soup.

The big soup spoon was just leaving my mouth when the twisted thought popped into my head again. I looked at Mallory. She was laughing because she saw I was trying not to. I tried to swallow, then heard Mallory laughing.

That's when Boston Clam Chowder sprayed out like birdshot from a shotgun, with clam bits and potato chunks cascading in two directions – one at Jackson, one at Lisa.

I still had some chowder in my mouth until I looked up and saw Lisa's chowder-covered leather jacket. I was going to say, "Have you been with another guy?"

Once that thought crossed my mind, the rest of the chowder flew out of my mouth and sprayed everyone else on that side of the table. There was chowder on everything, and I wasn't sure if the stuff on my face came from my mouth or my nose, or if it was even chowder.

That's why the manager wanted to have a word with us, but he never figured out what to say. So, he left, probably wishing he'd never come in the first place.

Unfortunately for him, he had to come back, this time with the rolls.

He gave me a snooty look while looking for a place on the table for the rolls amid the debris of food pieces and spitballs. Finally,

28

he cleared a spot. I waited till he set them down then said, "No thanks we're good."

My mom wasn't entirely right when she told the manager we were celebrating. It was more of a much-needed release for a family that had been through the wringer of, among other things, addiction. The manager didn't need know that, but he must have wondered how much worse it would have been if we'd been drinking.

If I were still drinking, our group wouldn't have been there. My near-fatal withdrawal in the hospital was ninety-six days earlier and, when my mom and aunt pulled me out of the lake house, I didn't have that many days of living left. I would hope my family wouldn't be at the Olive Garden laughing and shooting spitballs.

MOST ALCOHOLICS – even the recovering ones – *especially* the recovering ones -- hate major holidays because that's when their drinking was on full display. It was always hard to sneak drinks when the family was opening presents, eating for five hours and playing Pictionary.

Even if you're as good at sneaking drinks as I was, it sucks to be DWAS – (Drunk While Acting Sober).

Alcoholics are no different than anyone else. They are endowed by their Creator with certain unalienable Rights, that among them is the freedom to drink and act as drunk as you are. Holidays rob them of that freedom.

For an alcoholic, Thanksgiving is especially evil. They get bullied into eating at noon with the rest of the family and for the rest of the day, they're too bloated to get drunk.

My family was probably worried. I'm sure the usual questions were running through their minds: *Will he be irritable and depressed? Is he going to want to leave? Will he disappear into the bathroom with a pint of vodka?*

Maybe I went overboard, but I was hell bent on showing them I was fine. I may have been confused, but I was lucid enough to throw food and piss off a restaurant manager. And, even though I was sober, I could still make them laugh.

Chapter Three

Da Nile is More Than a River

TWO MONTHS AFTER REHAB

At Alcoholics Anonymous meetings, my resume of violent and erratic behavior barely raises an eyebrow. Somewhere in the room, at least one person will be nodding their head in agreement. I remember talking about my barely-provoked attack on my ex-wife's lawyer in open court.

I was worried about sharing that story because I didn't want everyone to think I was a raging thug. Halfway through the story, I saw Dean in the back of the room, nodding in agreement, probably because I was talking about physically assaulting a lawyer.

Dean is an old-timer who describes himself as an "old South Street drunk." I doubt anyone has ever looked at him and disputed the accuracy of that description. He's clearly thrown a few punches in his day.

He has a rep in the Glens Falls area... and I don't mean representative. It's probably not as bad as my reputation in

Albany, Chestertown and Guilderland – but I can usually count on him for empathy when I'm talking about my violent past.

I never drank on South Street, but I can picture Dean drinking there, at the end of the bar, harassing everyone within earshot. He's not mean; he's straight forward, like Harry Truman in a flannel shirt with a touch of Archie Bunker thrown in for political balance.

I'm not sure what it is – a secret cologne maybe – but Dean attracts the women. They trust him, and they can. He flirts, but he does it with fatherly respect and he'd be the first one to come charging to their rescue if they needed help.

These are just my observations about friends -- observations that are freely available outside the sanctuary of AA anonymity. In other words, they're fair game.

Still, I'll catch some heat from the AA sticklers and purists. The good news is that I don't care.

I don't see Alcoholics Anonymous as a righteous cult with a secret handshake and a million bylaws. For me, it's a fun place where I've watched people heal and grow.

These days, I don't question myself very often. I'm sober, so I assume I'm making the right decisions or what I think are the right decisions, which, in my mind, is the same thing.

There's nothing wrong with talking about general things that happen in the rooms of AA. Breaking anonymity, which I would never do, is one of the few principles of the program I consider inviolable.

Everything else is just a matter of showing respect and gratitude where it's due.

A perfect example is Boon, who looked like the front man for a gang of outlaw bikers. Boon had the voice of a guy who was trying to conserve air.

Whenever he said, "Back in the day," which was a lot, it came out as a single, four syllable word. His words shot out like bullets from a semiautomatic rifle – in rapid, rhythmic bursts.

I'm not an expert on pentameter, but I think Boon spoke in blank verse unrhymed iambic pentameter:

*I-aint-gonna **LIE**,*
*I-had-a-good **TIME**,*
Back-in-the-day.

I was happy when Boon showed up an hour early for a meeting in Glens Falls one morning. I was there an hour beforehand to make coffee, something I'd done there for three years.

"You came early to help me make coffee?" I asked him.

"No, but I'll help you put out some of these chairs," he said.

He put down one chair, then sat on it.

I don't confide in people outside my family. I talk to my mom and Lisa and sometimes Charles. I'll share little problems.

The windshield wiper fluid in my Kia is constantly freezing up. One night, I swallowed my pride and sought guidance on what to do about that from Chad, one AA's great purveyors of sage advice.

"Pour warm water on the little holes where the fluid sprays out," he told me.

I could have done that, I suppose. Instead, I waited until the weather got warmer. That worked too.

Maybe that's why I don't confide in people – I ignore their advice.

Boon walked in after I'd spent the night worrying about Jackson, who'd been in a rut of depression for months. I was reading and re-reading Jackson's texts to me, psychoanalyzing every word and getting myself all worked up in a frenzy of stupid and irrational thoughts.

Boon helped me snap out of it.

"Seriously," I asked him. "Why are you here so early?"

"Came to see you. How ya doing? Everything alright?"

"Let me run something by you," I said.

"What's on your mind?"

I gave him the facts first, then told him about all the worst-case scenarios I had concocted in my head. He just listened, and I could tell from his eyes that he was contemplating everything I was telling him.

As I was unloading everything from my head, I started to realize, just by hearing myself out loud, that I'd been blowing things out of proportion and driving myself crazy.

When I finished, Boon was quick to confirm it for me.

"Sounds like you've spent a lot of time in your own head."

"Am I overthinking it and getting carried away?"

"That's what alcoholics do. We get all wound up."

Yes, we do -- over everything, from matters of life and death to the silliest and stickiest of situations.

Fortunately, I had a medical doctor – a psychiatrist – who understood alcoholism and all the bizarre, post-rehab stuff I was experiencing -- the confusion, the mood swings, the delusions.

Did I mention the delusions?

In case you missed it, I made a point of distinguishing a psychiatrist from a psychologist. I've never wanted therapy. It's just not my thing. My mom advocates it, but the kind of help I needed after rehab was recognizing the symptoms of Post-Acute-Withdrawal Syndrome. That's a medical issue.

For all other issues, there's Alcoholics Anonymous. For occasional guidance, I have a sponsor.

I would never completely pour my heart out to anyone. Some cards aren't meant to be played.

Besides, real men don't get on the couch. It means you wanna kiss other boys.

Did I mention the delusions?

DR. STILLER AND I have an unusual history. I first met him at the psychiatric facility I was mandated to after overdosing on Klonopin in 2003. He was the psychiatrist in charge of the treatment team there. They treated him like a God. I didn't like

35

him, but it's hard to like anyone when you're locked in a mental unit.

Once a week, they called me into a room with a big conference table, and I had to sit front and center while Stiller and a team of therapists and counselors asked me questions about my feelings.

In my world, that's like being waterboarded.

Maybe that's why I'm not a champion of therapy and other forms of emotional healing. Once something has been forced on you, it's hard to embrace it when you have a choice. If you spend a few months in jail, you won't be looking for a bologna sandwich when you get out.

The therapy roundtable sessions were excruciating. I'd have rather have spent the hour watching tanks driving over a field of puppies.

I got through the sessions with a visualization technique that, ironically, I learned the day before. Each time one of them asked me a question, I'd visualize myself killing them.

I never shared that feeling with them. Like I said, some cards aren't meant to be played.

Stiller was the worst one in the group because he never said anything. He just stared right through me, then looked down at his notepad like he was trying to think of words stupid enough to describe what I just said. Then he'd tilt his head a little and jot something down.

I wanted to snatch his little pen and write FUCK YOURSELF on his forehead.

36

So, it may seem a little weird that he's been my doctor ever since.

When I left the psychiatric center, the staff there put Stiller down as my temporary primary care physician. They gave me a list of doctors who could take me on permanently. For fifteen years, I've been forgetting to do that.

I misjudged Stiller back in 2003. It's not that I didn't like *him*; I didn't like the truth and he was the one who kept telling it to me.

I knew things wouldn't be normal for me when I got out of rehab in 2013. I'd spent the past twenty-five years in three states: 1) drunk; 2) drinking but not drunk yet; 3) sober and figuring out how to get drunk.

In the year before rehab, I was drunk 24/7. For that entire year, I couldn't have passed a breathalyzer test at any point of any day.

Twenty-eight days in rehab wasn't going to reverse twenty-six years of damage. It would take time. I understood that. But I still didn't like or believe Stiller's diagnosis when I met with him a week after leaving St. Mary's.

"I can't remember anything," I told him. "Everything is fuzzy, and I feel like I'm in a walking coma."

"That'll clear up, but it's going to take some time," he said.

"Another month?"

"Be prepared for another year."

He's good at just saying shit like that without worrying about how I'm going to like it.

"A year? No way. It only took me about a month the last time," I told him.

"That was ten years and six rehabs ago," he said. "The progression of this disease almost killed you. When you left the Caron Foundation, we thought you were dead."

I was positive he was wrong. I left his office selling my own theories to myself.

How would he know? He's probably never even been drunk. It'll take fifty days. That's two days sober to recover from every one year of being drunk.

I actually convinced myself that that made sense. I kept repeating it to myself as I walked around the parking lot looking for the blue Dodge Charger I traded in the year before.

The car thing was a recurring problem. For some reason, I just couldn't remember that my car was a white Chevy Impala. I was always looking for that rolling felony of a Dodge Charger I used to own.

But I was living the dream, walking in circles wherever I went, shaking for no reason, sweating in cold weather, stuttering like… a stutterer, and having irrational thoughts and ideas.

There were a lot of little things too, weird stuff.

Until I got sober, I didn't realize I had so many pet peeves. I'm not sure where they came from, how they developed or what they mean. A lot of them have to do with food, which doesn't seem to have any special meaning in my life.

The one thing they have in common is that they're all weird. I'm almost embarrassed to write about them, but I haven't invoked the fifth amendment about anything else, so here we go:

I don't like people who wear their cell phones on their belt.

I don't like people who drive maroon Saturn's.

I hate when people try to win an argument with the snotty phrase, "That little thing called the Constitution."

I don't like it when construction workers have a small coffee and one donut.

I hate it when guys use their thumb and index finger to show you how thick their steak was the night before, especially if they say, "It was ye thick!"

I hate it when people go on a cruise and take pictures of the ice sculptures on the buffet table, and I hate when they caption the photo with, "Look at this spread!"

Certain words bother me to the point of making me mad. I don't know what it is, but I think Dr. Miller does.

The words fall into three categories:

Words I don't like: *refreshments, pupil, varicose, feast, savvy, goodies, garnish, gout, refurbish and bowel;*

Words I hate: *Impervious, portion, epic, squamous, vagina (but don't get me wrong), alumnus, snuggle and stool;*

Words that make me want to drink again: *tasty, moist, yummy, larvae, cozy, cuddle and ointment.*

These are the kinds of conversations I was having with Stiller – although, they weren't really conversations because I was doing all the talking.

He seemed interested in hearing it all, and he occasionally jotted something down on his notepad. He was probably alphabetizing the list of medications I was going to need.

I didn't know it at the time, but my mother and Lisa were feeding him additional information behind my back.

The day those two women joined forces was the day I officially surrendered control of my own destiny – which is fine because, look what I did with it.

For the first time, Stiller saw what my normal was. In other words, he saw what I was like without alcohol in my life.

Looking back on it now, I don't think my normal was normal.

Apparently, neither did Stiller. After seven months of analyzing, he'd heard enough to make some significant adjustments to my regimen of medication.

It jumped from one medication for sleep to four medications for… whatever. I'm sure we discussed it, and I'm equally sure I didn't listen. I don't ask questions if I know I'm going to hate the answers. Just give me the medicine. I don't need the brochure.

That may sound neglectful on my part, but I'd spent the past ten years in and out of more than a dozen different hospitals, mental health units and rehabs. My medications were changing every week. Doctors and nurse practitioners got carpel tunnel syndrome writing and rewriting my prescriptions.

In those settings, you don't ask questions about bloating or irritability or even diagnoses. You just take the medicine and hope it gives you a nice buzz. I stopped asking questions around the time I stopped caring, which was close to the beginning.

Stiller could be sitting five feet away from me with the answer to a question that's burning in my mind. Instead of asking, I'll go home and search for clues about what the answer *might* be.

Why? Because I don't want a definite answer; I want a couple of options. That way, I can satisfy my curiosity and still have a denial mechanism in place if the clue leans toward the answer I don't want.

So, I went home and Googled my medications.

Nine out of ten times, that's a bad idea. Most Google searches lead to inoperable cancer. Mine led to crazy, so I just closed out of the page and went to Dunkin Donuts.

But, the subject of crazy came up again in the summer of 2014.

It was my first summer since leaving rehab, and I spent most of it up at the lake house with Jackson and Michael. I was looking for fireworks to blow off on the Fourth of July, when I realized something was missing from the closet where I used to keep the guns.

Yeah, the guns.

I stepped back, gawking at the empty corner of the closet where the four guns were lined up the last time I saw them. I should have been going nuts and calling the police, but something in the back of my mind, a crux of a memory, was keeping me in check.

Then it all came back to me. There was no point in going crazy and calling the police. The police already thought I was crazy, which is why they took the guns in the first place.

I remembered *what* happened very clearly -- I just forgot *that* it happened.

Nothing precipitated the whole thing. I didn't walk outside and start shooting. I didn't threaten to kill anyone. I didn't say I wanted to kill the President. Hell, I probably didn't know who the President was.

I guess it's wrong to say nothing precipitated the whole thing. Obviously, *something* happened that winter night in 2012, when a few police cars rolled up to the house just before midnight.

To this day, I don't know what it was.

It wasn't unusual for the police to visit my house, but I usually had some idea why they were there. This time, as I watched them walk up the driveway, I was racking my brain, trying to remember what I did, when I did it, and what the statute of limitations was.

I couldn't think of anything that would warrant this degree of police attention but, speaking of warrants, they had one.

I didn't wait for the officers on the porch to start pounding on the door. I wanted to be proactive, so I locked Bam in my bedroom and greeted them on the porch.

"Hi, I've been here all night. It couldn't have been me. My daughter is upstairs, and I haven't left her all night."

Apparently, they didn't need any of that information.

"Where's your German Shepard?"

"Bam? He's locked in my bedroom."

"How about your guns? Where are those?"

"Oh, don't worry about my guns," I said. "They're in the bedroom with Bam."

"We're going to need to look at those."

At that point, it was safe to let Bam out. Once people have made it past the door, Bam assumes I want them there, which I didn't, but there wasn't anything Bam or I could do about it.

"They're all legally registered," I told them.

"We know they're registered," one officer said, as two others began pulling guns out of my bedroom closet.

It was one of the few times in my life when being drunk was a good thing. If I had been sober, there's not a chance in hell I would have made their jobs this easy.

For starters, I would have demanded to know why they were there at the door instead of in the living room. If they said, "Yeah, we're just here to confiscate your guns," I might have gone full-scale Ruby Ridge on their asses.

The sober me was *that* unpredictable. I have two copies of the constitution right near the door. At the very least, I would have whipped out one of those and asserted myself intellectually. At the very worst, I would have drawn a red line at the front door and asserted myself stupidly.

I would have lost either way. It's just a matter of how badly I would have lost.

Like I said, it's a good thing I was drunk enough to not care. I just sat at my desk saying quippy things as the officers laid my guns out on my favorite couch.

"Spread out, make yourself at home," I told them.

What pissed me off is that Bam was hanging out with them like he was on their K9 unit. They were petting him.

"You're not gonna take him too, are you?"

"We'd love to," one of them said, while patting Bam on the head. "He'll be a great K-9."

Two years later, I still had Bam, but I was having a tough time swallowing the confiscation of my guns. I was retroactively furious. I stood there, staring at that empty closet.

That night, I went to a meeting twenty minutes from the lake house -- in the middle of nowhere – that I'd never been to. I didn't know anyone.

The great thing about AA is I can walk into a meeting anywhere in the world and talk about what happened earlier – how I stood in front of the closet, clueless about where my guns had gone – and no one is going to be shocked.

No one is going to stand up and yell, "How in the hell could you forget that the police seized your guns?" Most of them have had something of theirs seized by the police, whether it's car, drugs or children.

"It literally took me three years to remember the police coming to the house and confiscating them," I told them.

Only one person in the group looked even slightly surprised, and he came up to me after the meeting.

"Stone Lake Road, right?"

"Yeah, in Chestertown."

"I probably shouldn't be telling you this, but I was one of the deputies that night taking the guns."

He was right; he shouldn't have told me.

"When are you bringing them back?" I asked, half-jokingly and half waiting for a fucking answer.

We talked about it for a few minutes and I was civil, but the constitutionalist in me was still outraged at having the government seizing my firearms.

Here's the thing: It's hard to assert your rights when you can't remember why you think they were violated.

And here's another thing: Warren County isn't Russia or even California (it's a joke, settle down). If the police took the draconian step of seizing my guns, I must have done something really fucked up. Did I really want the details? No, I didn't. But, as usual, I wanted a clue.

So, when the cop at the meeting told me I should call the County property room and ask if I could have my guns back, I reluctantly made the call the next morning.

It was a conversation for the ages.

"Hi, my name is John Wolfe and I'm calling about some guns I have there."

"Yes, I know who you are," he said. "You're going to need a note from a doctor stating that you're of sound mind and not a danger to yourself or others."

"No doctor is going to write me a letter like that."

"No, they're not."

Wow! That was quick.

"Excuse me? What makes you say… never mind."

I couldn't click off that page fast enough. Just as it was with my medications, I could tell I was about to get an answer I didn't like, so it was time to hang up the phone.

I didn't get out of it with my ego unscathed, though. Warren County is huge. Yet, both he and another sheriff in a town thirty miles away knew who I was? Was I *that* bad? I've never even been arrested… at least, not in Warren County.

At first, I wasn't going to bother asking Dr. Stiller for a letter. It would have been devastating to get the same answer twice. An anonymous verdict from such a wide spectrum of opinions – from clinical to legal – would devastate my ego.

But, again, I couldn't resist looking for a clue about what he *might* say.

At my next appointment, I told Stiller about the guns and what the Property Clerk said. It was another unfortunate response that appeared to be heading south.

46

"Can you believe that?" I asked.

Stiller stared at me. His head was moving so slightly, I couldn't tell if he was nodding a *yes*, or shaking a *no*.

Oh crap, I think he's nodding!

I quickly changed the subject.

Rationalizing this one was a no-brainer. It's not that Stiller thought I was crazy or that I would ever shoot anyone. He probably would have volunteered to write the note, I told myself, if there wasn't such a whopping liability issue.

If he wrote a letter predicting I would never shoot someone, his insurance company would shoot both of us. That's all it was... most likely.

With only two months of sobriety, I had to keep reminding myself that the only thing on my priority list should be going to meetings, relearning basic living skills and trying to reclaim my faculties. Guns shouldn't even be on the list.

Every day, I was being reminded why.

THE PARKING LOT OF SAINT MICHAEL'S Church was jammed when I pulled in for the eleven o'clock meeting. That usually meant there was a funeral underway and it was going to be a pain in the ass to find a spot -- and an even bigger pain in the ass to get out at noon when everyone was leaving.

No offense to the dearly departed, but once you're dead, you should really stay the hell out of everyone's way. You had your time. Now, you're trying to ruin the time *we* have left.

Thoughts like that popped into my head a hundred times a day during my first year of sobriety. It was a scary and controversial place, my mind.

I left the meeting five minutes early to avoid the mass exodus of mourners in the parking lot – but it was already underway by the time I got to my car.

There were cars scattered all over the place. It looked like God took a handful of cars and threw them down like grass seed onto the parking lot.

It was the kind of scene you should expect to see when two hundred people over the age of eighty put on their little tweed driving hats, ease themselves into their cars and drive with their turn signals on all the way to the church.

The real chaos comes when all those Buicks, with their Triple A stickers, converge on one parking lot at the same time. That's what was brewing in my head as I was trying to find a way out of the parking lot.

There was no way to get to the exits, so I drove behind the church.

You'd have to see the layout of the parking lot to appreciate what a stupid idea that was. It's like waiting in line at the front door, then running around the building and getting back in the same line.

So, now I'm the one with the tweed hat, driving along this narrow little road behind the church. That's when a guy in a black suit started waving me into a lane of traffic cones. At first, I thought he was trying to expedite the flow of traffic out of the parking lot.

Then I realized I was the fifth car in a growing line of vehicles with their headlights on. At the front of the line were two hearses.

Not only was I in a funeral procession, I was at the front of it with the family members of the deceased. I got such a prominent place in the procession because, like a dumb ass, I left the meeting five minutes early, and so did the grieving family members.

I couldn't escape. The guy in the black suit had me packed in there nice and tight, bumper to bumper, with traffic cones on both sides.

After a few minutes, there was at least thirty cars lined up behind me. And now, the main parking lot had cleared out. I could see the guys from the meeting driving away. All the cars that were jammed in the parking lot an hour ago were in the procession with me.

A whistle blew and two guys in black suits began waving the hearses and the rest of the procession forward to Route 9.

The hearses were turning left, and I figured that would be my opportunity to break free from the procession by turning right. Nope.

The motorcycle cop with the puffy pants and the whistle wasn't going to let it happen. He had his motorcycle parked in the middle of the road so the old people in the procession couldn't screw up and turn right. He had us marching in formation like penguins. I was going left, whether I liked it or not.

Out of respect, I turned on my headlights.

We drove about twenty-five miles per hour up Route 9, from South Glens Falls to Glens Falls and, eventually, to Queensbury. I was going to the gym in Queensbury anyway, so I just stayed in line with my lights on and let the motorcycle cop wave me through the red lights.

Onlookers from cars going in the other direction gave us sympathetic smiles, especially those of us at the front of the procession who were grieving the most.

We passed Crandall Park on the left, then wound our way into the commercial district of Queensbury where Route 9 turns into two lanes.

I knew it was time to say goodbye.

I was no longer mad at the dead guy for inconveniencing me, especially because I made it quicker to the gym than I would have if he'd never died. Thank you, sir.

As the procession moved into the right line towards Pine View Cemetery, I wondered how bewildered the other mourners were going to be when I suddenly bolted and said, "Fuck this! I'm going to the gym."

I had endured all seven stages of grief in eighteen minutes. Shock and denial were now acceptance and hope.

We all have a...

Okay, enough of that.

MOST PEOPLE LOSE their ability to do simple things when they're drunk. For me, it was the other way around. I couldn't even ditch a funeral procession.

At some point in the early 90s, I started drinking alcoholically.

About ten years later, in the early 2000s, I not only needed alcohol to be happy, I needed it to be functional. I relied on it to perform daily tasks, like writing and talking.

I was always so drunk, I got used to doing everything that way.

When I left rehab in October of 2013, Lisa got the opposite of what she was expecting. Instead of being, energetic, confident and sharp, I was clumsy, incompetent and dumb. She was expecting Tom Brady; she got James Brady.

That was awful, and I apologize.

I laugh about my oblivious, incompetent and neurotic conduct now, but when it was happening, I would have pushed a button to vaporize myself if one were available. I wouldn't have killed myself, but I was all for the vaporization thing.

Walking around without yourself for an entire year is demoralizing. It's hard to feel good about your sobriety when you can't remember which way to turn out of the driveway.

Every time something like that happened, I promised myself that, if my world didn't clear up the very next morning, I'd clear it up myself with thirty beers and a bottle of vodka.

I was having delusions and paranoia, both of which can be fatal in a person with a proclivity for violence.

For about three hundred mornings in a row, I woke up feeling worse than my nastiest hangover. Each morning, I decided to give it "one more day."

I didn't realize it at the time, but I was going to have to learn everything all over again. If I had known that, I probably would have said... well, I'm not sure *what* I would have said but it wouldn't have been the serenity prayer.

There are varying degrees of confusion, varying degrees of obliviousness and varying degrees of stupid. My post-rehab conduct covered the entire spectrums of all three. And many times, I dragged otherwise normal people right down to my level.

All along, the plan was for me to move in with Lisa and her kids after rehab. I just don't remember whose plan it was. We weren't married yet, just engaged, so it wasn't an automatic thing.

The contrast between their world and any world I had ever lived in couldn't have been greater.

The O'Donnell house was G-rated in every sense of the term, and the outside world was parentally-blocked.

The only TV show they watched was *Full House* – and they thought it was hilarious.

Profanity was prohibited, and "damn" was profanity.

They wore safety glasses to sharpen a pencil.

Social Media? No way. Too much bullying out there.

I'm not mocking my wife... wait, I am. What I mean is, I'm not *criticizing* her. Mothers are supposed to be protective.

I just never understood why such a protective mother would invite me into the house. Wouldn't it be safer to take in bail jumpers and recovering pimps?

The second I walked in the door, all of Lisa's positive influence shot right out the window.

A hundred times a day, you'd hear one of her children say, "What's he doing, Mother? I'm frightened."

Don't drop the book and call CPS. It's a joke… pretty much.

Mallory and Jackson grew up with me. They've seen their fair share of blood, sweat and tears. Hell, they've seen their dad on fire. In other words, they've heard me say "damn."

Michael and Rachel, on the other hand, were unseasoned and, well, delicate – but they weren't going to stay that way very long.

Now that Bam and I were in the house, they'd have to endure loud barking, vicious growling and having food snapped out of their hands. They'd also have to deal with Bam.

So, the whole merging process could only go one of two ways. Someone was going to have to change. Either they could turn me, or I could turn them.

How do you think that worked out? With me sitting in front of the TV with a bowl of unsalted popcorn, giggling every time one of the adorable Olson twins says "dude"?

Right after Lisa and I got married in 2014, I came up with the ultimate prank. I'd wait about a year until everyone in the house was acting just like me.

Michael would get suspended from school for fighting, then spend his days pulling down trees in the backyard with the neighbor's truck. Rachel would be running around the house screaming, "Mom, where the fuck did you put my vape?"

Once I corrupted everyone and everything in the house, I'd pack up and leave.

Lisa didn't think it was funny either.

Chapter Four

Sushi Over Strawberries

As I was leaving St. Mary's, a nurse gave me a hug then pinched my chest.

"Don't take life so seriously," she told me.

"No one's ever accused me of that."

If that's all I had to do to survive, recovery was going to be a breeze. Not taking life seriously was my specialty. Doing it the other way around is what always got me in trouble.

When Mallory was eleven, I waited in her school's bus loop to confront a bus driver who was being inappropriate with her.

By the time it was over, cops were everywhere, and the school was in lockdown.

The following year, I learned that my ex-wife's boyfriend was yelling and swearing at Mallory.

By the time *that* holy mess was over, he was hiding behind a stack of protective orders and I was arrested repeatedly for ignoring every one of them.

When Mallory was sixteen, three guys in a local bar made a vulgar comment about her. (She wasn't in the bar, obviously.) By the time *that* was over, two of the guys were lying in a pool of blood and the police were outside my house with bullhorns.

The point is, I have a history. I'm a protective father. Some would say I'm an overprotective father. Others would say I'm something worse than that, like the Guilderland Police, the State Police, the Warren County Police, and judiciary staffs of Albany, Schenectady and Warren Counties.

Mallory and Jackson didn't condemn me for it, so I really don't care what anyone else thinks.

Even the police seemed to have empathy, which is why I wiggled out of handcuffs in Town courts from Albany to Guilderland to Queensbury to Chestertown -- without ever going to prison.

I may have been guilty *ipso facto*, but I wasn't acting out of maliciousness or greed or bravado. I just lost control while trying to protect my kids, and I'll never – never -- apologize to anyone other than them for that.

I wasn't going to stay sober very long if I didn't change that part of me.

For Mallory's sake, I had to find a way.

In January of 2014, about three months after I left rehab, Mallory broke up with her jealous, abusive boyfriend.

Days later, while she was picking up her things at his house, he lost his temper, grabbed hold of her and said she wasn't going anywhere.

When she tried to leave, he blocked the door.

When Mallory fought to get out, he pinned her down. He was screaming incoherently at the top of his lungs. Mallory must have been horrified, but she had the presence of mind to record the assault.

She fought for several minutes, but her weightlifting ex-boyfriend overpowered her.

What happened after that was awful and against her will. I heard the tape. The police heard the tape. The guy sounded insane, insane enough to kill her.

I can't imagine what was going through my daughter's mind.

This time, Mallory needed a father, not a hit man. She told me – firmly – to let her and the police handle it. The last thing she needed was me acting like me.

It didn't matter what I wanted to do. The only thing that mattered is doing exactly what Mallory needed me to do.

This time, being strong meant the opposite of what it used to mean. I'm not sure why something so simple took me so long to understand.

How could I be there for Mallory if I was off looking for someone to kill? How could I comfort her if I was adding to her discomfort?

We talked, but mostly, I listened. If I had vented my anger to her, she wouldn't have been free to show her sadness to me.

A day later, she did. It was wrenching. I've never felt so helpless, but I've also never been so proud of my daughter.

In the end, Mallory dealt with it the way she deals with everything... her way. She knew what needed to happen for her to move on, then she made it happen. Through that process, I realized that I don't just love my daughter, I look up to her.

IN AA, THEY TALK ABOUT "living life on life's terms." Mallory lives life on Mallory's terms.

About two years after the ordeal, she called me in the middle of the day. With Mallory, it's never a routine call because, in her world, nothing is ever routine. Something's always going on and it's always unexpected.

Where are you?" I asked.

"Having lunch at a Chinese restaurant."

"You went to a Chinese restaurant by yourself?"

"It was all you can eat sushi."

Mallory doesn't give a shit what other people think about her for eating alone. She saw a sign saying she could eat all the sushi she wanted for one low price, and she barged in and started devouring fish.

But that's not why she called.

"I joined the basketball team."

She knows I hate the sound of people eating, so she was chomping on the fish as loud as she could.

"You don't even play basketball."

"That's why I joined. I wanna learn and get good at it."

58

Mallory started calling me on the way home from her basketball practices.

"I'm a good rebounder," she told me. "I'm still working on my dribbling because you have to keep doing that when you run with the ball. You're not allowed to stop."

"Yeah, that's one of the rules..."

"Oh, and our first game is next week," she said.

"I'm really proud of you, honey. Can I ask you a question?"

"Yeah."

"What are you going to do if they put you in the game?"

"I'll cry."

When I saw Mallory in her basketball uniform for the first time, I sat in the stands thinking: This is an actual college basketball game. The other girls are real basketball players, and they're twice Mallory's size.

Mallory looked so cool on the bench, cheering on her team. About ten minutes into the game, she ran out onto the court to guard a girl who was almost a foot taller than her and looked like she could kick my ass. My heart was racing. I was scared.

Mallory wasn't. She defended the basket like it had her life's savings in it, crouching down in the defensive position, waiting for someone to bring it, as I yelled her name from the stands, clapping my hands and stomping on the floor boards when she got her first rebound.

FOR A LONG TIME after the attack on Mallory, I felt like I failed her because the guy who did this to her is still breathing. For as long as Mallory and Jackson have been alive, I've sworn on everything holy to me that if someone ever did something like this to them, I would gladly take the twenty-five years in prison for killing whoever did it.

Mallory killed him herself, in a way that was more swift and severe than anything I could have done – and without all the violence and chaos. She got her Licensed Massage Therapist license, made her college basketball team and she's getting a degree in criminal justice. At last check, she had a 3.9 grade point average at Schenectady Community College.

Nothing I've ever done in her defense is better than that. It just felt good at the time. I now realize that all the hell raised on Mallory and Jackson's behalf in the past was aimed at solving my problem more than theirs.

A lot of women like to portray themselves as strong and independent, totally unconcerned about being judged by others. I see their memes on Facebook. It's usually a picture of an attractive, carefree-looking woman sitting back on a recliner with her feet up, eating strawberries and enjoying the sunset. Superimposed over that will be something like: *I've reached that point in life where I don't really care what other people think.*

Bullshit. If you weren't worried about what other people thought, you wouldn't bother to advertise it

Drop the strawberries and lose the sunset. Go to the nearest sushi dive and cram raw fish in your mouth. Then I'll believe you don't care what other people think.

Chapter Five

"Death is Funny"

Alcoholics don't heal quickly. As evidence, I offer the title of this chapter. It's in quotes for a reason -- and, as much as I'd prefer to attribute it to someone else, how could I deny myself the glory?

I don't embarrass easily. I'll run through a crowded mall yelling "Death is funny" without being embarrassed. Who cares? People would think I was back on drugs, and the joke would be on them because I was an alcoholic, not an addict.

The problem is context. Not only was I serious when I said death was funny, I was trying to boost the morale of young people. Yeah, that's where it makes you cringe.

I had been in AA for about four months. There was only one meeting in the Glens Falls area where there were a lot of people newer than me – mostly young people from one of two halfway houses.

In other words, at least once a week, I wasn't the most fucked up person in the room – until I was.

I forgot what the topic of discussion was that day. It wasn't "The Funny Thing About Being Dead" -- at least, not until I opened my big fat mouth.

"In 2003, my heart stopped beating twice and I was on life support at Albany Med. I died, twice. Is it funny? Kinda."

Sum stultus. That's Latin for "I'm an idiot."

About ten minutes later, a girl talked about a friend of hers that got killed. She kept looking at me while she was telling the story about how it happened – almost like she was daring me to laugh about the funny death of her friend.

I can tell when someone is lying, and I can also tell when someone is trying to make a point. This girl was doing both.

Most things are tolerated in AA. There are no rules, per se. You can vent. You can be wrong. You can whine. You can say death is funny. You can even walk into the room bombed. None of that will get you thrown out of an AA meeting.

In fact, you don't really have to be an alcoholic to be in AA. You're supposed to be, but it's not like there's someone standing at the door with a blood test. There's not a secret handshake. We can't tell by looking at you.

In the beginning, I had to learn that not everyone drank like me. I had to realize that not all alcoholics started drinking at eight o'clock in the morning.

I had to tolerate the "horror stories" of high bottom alcoholics who said things like, "On a hot summer day, what good is a pizza without a nice cold can of beer?"

What the hell is a "Can of beer?" It sounds like something the Queen of England would ask for at a coal miners picnic.

Alcoholics don't drink cans of beer. We drink cases of beer. We don't drink bottles of Budweiser. We drink bottles of vodka.

And what's up with the "hot summer day" thing? Unless there's a blizzard keeping us away from the beer store, alcoholics don't give a fuck what it's doing outside.

We drink the same amount of booze on a hot summer day as we do in a Category Five hurricane. Beer isn't a thirst-quencher.

We don't mix beer with pizza; we mix it with vodka. Why would you ruin alcohol with food?

As for "Nice cold beer," the temperature of a beer doesn't change the alcohol content, which is the only thing that matters.

Alcoholics will drink warm beer, cheap beer, flat beer and expired beer. We will drink the beer that everyone else throws away.

I drank more than thirty beers every day for a long time. Why? Because I loved the taste? Fuck no. Dr. Pepper tastes a hundred times better than beer, but it won't get me drunk.

Towards the end of my drinking career, I'd get to the convenience store at 7:45 am and count down the seconds to 8:00 am when it was legal to buy a thirty-pack. Most alcoholics didn't do that. Most alcoholics tackled the problem when they found themselves drinking every day. They didn't wait till they were drinking every hour.

Most alcoholics didn't have to go rehab, much less seven of them.

Here's the thing. The rooms of AA are the only place where a guy like me can say that death is funny, and a woman can say she likes a cold beer on a summer day – and he thinks *she's* the weird one.

Some people need alcohol in their lives. They need it to "fit in." I drank alone. There was no one to fit in *with.* Some people need "a few drinks" before they go out bar hopping. I needed it before I went to the liquor store.

I don't need it anymore, but I do need regular interaction with people who have the disease of alcoholism, no matter how much or how little they drank.

As for death being funny... that was just the lingering vapors of a million beers talking, although I can think of a few instances where it would be true.

I heard the story of an African ivory poacher being stomped to death by the elephant he was trying to kill. That's the funniest fucking thing I've heard in years. If there was a video of it, I'd keep it in my desk drawer and watch it every time I need cheering up.

The only way it could have been funnier is if the elephant ripped the guy's teeth out and carved them into tiny letter openers.

I died for over one minute and I didn't wake up laughing. Death isn't usually funny. I'm not sure why I told thirty people it was. The interesting thing is, I said death is funny and only one person offered a different opinion.

The different opinion came from the girl who talked about her "dead friend." She walked up to me after the meeting and got in my face.

"What the fuck! Death is funny?" she snapped.

"I meant yours, not mine."

I don't care how right you are and how wrong I am. If you come up to me with an attitude, I'm going to be a dick.

At the time, the whole concept of death being funny made perfect sense to me – not that I was crashing funerals and mocking people for crying, but I wasn't mourning with them either.

It's not that I'd lost my capacity to feel. I lost my ability to comprehend – and, a full six months after leaving rehab, I still hadn't got it back.

I don't feel that way anymore. Living is clearly better.

Still, when I die, I hope people laugh more than they cry. In my Will – which I clearly wrote when I was thoroughly shitfaced and delusional -- I requested the reading of "Invictus" at my funeral.

Timothy McVeigh asked prison officials to read the same poem before his execution. I should probably pick something else -- a limerick maybe, like the one about the man from Nantucket.

I hope they bring Sharpies to my wake and write stuff on my face, like "Insert penis here" with an arrow pointing to my mouth. You know how many times I've done that to other people? Not once has it been done to me. My wake is everyone's last chance.

It's better than hovering over me saying how good I look. Dead people don't look good; they look dead.

If you thought I was funny when I was alive, bring a sharpie to my wake. You can be sure that, by the time I die, there's not going to be anything in my Last Will and Testament about "Invictus."

"I am the master of my fate. I am the captain of my soul?"

I can't even cut my own steak. Bring the Sharpie.

Chapter Six

The 90s are Over

SIX MONTHS SOBER

Even after six months of being sober and going to AA meetings, I didn't have any friends. A few good people tried to befriend me, but I made it impossible. Every attempt to reach out to me was met with a stiff-arm. I was suspicious, unwilling and unready. Just talking to other people made me restless and uncomfortable.

I had extreme highs, like the night at the Olive Garden, but even the highs were a problem for me because I didn't feel like I was in control.

Most days, I didn't feel much better than I did when I walked out of rehab. I was still shaking, sweating and stuttering – and imagining things. Wherever I went, I felt like I was guilty of something... like I should be ashamed.

More than anything else, I was aloof and out of touch, like the rest of the world had a big meeting and I missed it, and now they were keeping a big secret from me.

I WALKED IN EARLY to a meeting one morning in Glens Falls. There was a group of ancient, John McCain-looking AA dudes in the corner. I didn't feel like talking to them, or anyone, so I pretended to read a newspaper that was on the table.

I wasn't really reading; I was eavesdropping, just to see what the Oldsmobile crowd talks about when their life is over because they can't drink anymore. It was morbid curiosity.

They were talking about the weather, ice fishing and prostates.

That's what scared me about AA and sobriety – boredom. I wasn't sure where I wanted to be in twenty or thirty years, but I didn't want to be in a corner talking about my prostate. I don't even know where my prostate is.

I kept eyeballing the door, praying that a group of young people would pour into the room so there'd be someone I could identify with – not that I'd bother talking to them.

As I was slowly flipping the newspaper pages, I saw the words, "Whitney Houston's estate." At first, I thought it was a reference to her mansion, but then I glanced at it a second time and saw something about her kids.

"Wait a minute," I said out loud. "Is Whitney Houston dead?"

The coffin-dodgers looked over at me, giggling like eight-year old girls. The oldest one in the group hacked out an answer.

"She's been dead for two years."

Another scrotum-faced retro piled on.

"And so is Michael Jackson... and Buddy Holly."

They continued to chuckle or cackle or whatever you call it when a bunch of antique alcoholics laugh at themselves.

I wanted to yell "Boo!" and send them all into cardiac arrest.

It's funny how life passes you by when you're alive but not really living. I had no idea Whitney Houston was dead.

That seems like pretty big news – not Princess Diana big, but certainly something people would be talking about for more than a few days. How could I have missed it? Was I *that* isolated from the outside world?

Then the door opened and a group of dudes in their twenties and thirties came in.

I thought, "Thank God, here come the boys."

They walked past my table and sat down about as far away from me as they could get. That's when it struck me: *Those aren't the boys anymore. Those were your boys two decades ago. Now, your boys are in the corner talking about their surgeries.*

Apparently, something happened while I was drunk and sequestered at the lake house: I stopped being young.

I remember celebrating my fortieth birthday up at the lake house by myself. For some reason, I decided to mark the occasion by frying a turkey on the back deck. For another unknown reason, I threw a chunk of snow into the boiling vat of oil and almost burned down the lake house.

I came damn close to celebrating my fiftieth birthday there too. God only knows how I would have celebrated that. I don't know how Lisa and Bam endured me.

I WAS ALMOST FIFTY and I had to accept it. I didn't want to be one of those people who refuse to act their age, especially the middle-aged parents who try to hang with their teenage kids and their friends.

They want to be known as "the cool parent," so they listen to their kids' music and act like the woman at Speedway who whispered sweet nothings in my ear one day.

"What the fuck already!"

No, seriously. She leaned forward and whispered that directly into my ear.

Ms. WTF was behind me in line at Speedway, and the woman in front of us was taking her sweet time deciding which scratch off tickets to buy next. Ms. Scratch Off played her first round of tickets right at the counter, then bought ten more tickets with the two dollars she won – without ever moving out of the way to let me and Ms. WTF buy our coffee.

I've found that the worst lines to wait in are the ones where lottery tickets are being sold or where the cashier needs a computer mouse to complete the transaction.

I had been waiting longer than Ms. WTF, but she was madder than I was.

She whispered in my ear again, this time a little louder.

"This bullshit has been going on – legit – ten minutes."

Legit? Was she still in high school? I still hadn't turned around to see what she looked like. I surmised she was one of those hip soccer moms who talks and dresses like her daughter's friends, so I turned around to see if I was right.

70

Yep, it was Cyndi Lauper trying to be Miley Cyrus -- pink hair, Pink brand sweats and a sweatshirt that read, "I Can't Pants Today."

Apparently, she couldn't toothbrush that day either.

If I was going to have that kind of mid-life crisis, I wouldn't even know who to talk and dress like. I can name exactly two young "artists" -- Cyrus and Justin Bieber. And the only reason I can name those two is because they're so stupid, it makes the evening news.

Having said all that, I'll admit this about the whole mid-life thing: Being in rehab – or, in my case, being in a lot of rehabs -- has a way of making you feel and act twenty years younger than you are.

It's a rude awakening when you get out of rehab and find a mailbox filled with shit from AARP. If you weren't in denial about your drinking, you're sure to be in denial about your age.

That's one of the few problems I didn't have. I knew I was going to be fifty soon. I didn't like it, but I didn't try to delay it by listening to the horrific whining noise they call music today.

But, Alcoholism has a way of time warping you, and I didn't even know what today's date was, much less today's music – or even yesterday's.

When I got into my car for the first time after rehab, my satellite radio settings had been erased. Before I left, every channel was set to classic rock from the 60s or the 70s.

Now, they were set to everything from bluegrass to salsa to "Forties on Four." For a while, I left it on the forties station. I liked it because I'd never heard most of it before, so it didn't bring back drunken memories.

Then I started to *like* it, like it. Artie Shaw became my favorite artist of the forties, along with Glen Miller, Ella Fitzgerald and that badass Lionel Hampton.

After a while, I wanted to hear other stuff too, but my brain was still too muddled to remember things like how to set the channels of a car radio. So, I just put it on "scan," and drove around listening to everything from big band and rock to country and rap... in ten second increments.

I did that for about two weeks until I had a giant meltdown and began poking the entire dashboard with all ten fingers until the medley from hell stopped somewhere tolerable.

It landed on the "Lithium" channel, which just happened to be playing a song I liked, so I left it there.

It turned out to be a station that played mostly new music, and I began eating my words because, well, I really liked it.

After a few months of listening to the Lithium channel, I felt like a kid again. I used to think that rock and roll was dead, but this new stuff sounded just as good as classic rock from the 70s. Some of it was even better.

I went on YouTube and played some of the songs I was hearing. There was this one kid I really liked – Bradley Nowell, the lead singer of a new band called Sublime.

I liked his style, running around with his Dalmatian, making music, living life hard and not giving a shit what anyone thought about it.

In a lot of ways, he reminded me of myself, and I vowed to go see this kid and his band if they ever got within five hundred miles of Glens Falls.

I was checking the band out online one night when I read Bradley Nowell's profile.

He'd been dead for over twenty years.

So... yeah.

Roger Daltrey of The Who will always be my favorite artist, but now Daltrey was my mother's age. I suppose that means he was always my mother's age.

It's just that, now, my mother and Daltrey are... let's just say it would be hard for the Who to perform *"My Generation"* anymore. It probably sounded cool to sing, *"I hope I die before I get old"* in 1966. It sounds a lot less cool to sing it in 2017, when you're seventy-two.

I mentioned Robin Williams in my first book. I liked him as much as anyone. I grew up with him. I wasn't a giant fan. I just liked him. I connected with him because of his disease, his addiction, and even his death. I identified with him.

Then there's Chris Cornell, the brilliant lead singer of Soundgarden.

The Lithium Channel brought me back to him. He was my age, one of the few artists whose voice was powerful enough to reach me when I was drinking.

Jackson has played guitar since he was ten years old. Today, it's his life, and it could very well be his career.

I always thought that, if he *did* make music his career, he would be a lot like Cornell. I couldn't put my finger on it but, even though Jackson was thirty-five years younger, they seemed to have an affinity of some kind.

It's a demeanor thing -- a certain, a certain... I feel like there's a French word I could use here, but I can't think of it and, besides, I don't want to sound like a pompous dick. It kinda rhymes with ménage à trois, but that's definitely not it. I'll stick with affinity.

SO, I'M DRIVING AROUND listening to the Lithium Channel when it finally sunk in – that it was 2014, and 90s music wasn't new anymore; it was just new to me.

I'd been so absorbed by, and in, alcohol, I hadn't changed a radio station in thirty years.

It wasn't just music. I was tuned out for so long, everything was unfamiliar and complicated when I finally tuned back in.

I was so socially unaware, I didn't know who was dead or who was alive. I didn't know if the Dead were still alive. I knew who was in the Who, but I forgot who in the Who was dead.

I knew Barack Obama was President, but I couldn't tell you who he beat to become President, or when Bush left office or who served as Vice President to either of them. And I *worked* in politics.

I started wondering what else I missed.

I found out the hard way, at the Philadelphia airport, that pay phones no longer exist. I had to ask some woman if I could use

74

her cell phone at the airport bar. Then she sat there and listened to me tell Charles that I just ran away from rehab.

And what happened to those blue postal drop boxes? They used to be on every other corner. Apparently, they disappeared with phone booths while I was shot-gunning beer and drinking vodka from a Poland Springs bottle.

Lisa asked me to mail something one morning. Our mailperson refused to take our outgoing mail because someone snapped our mailbox's little red flag in half.

Apparently, flying the red flag at half-mast isn't enough to catch her attention.

She told Lisa that, without the raised flag, there was no way for her to know whether a letter was outgoing mail or leftover mail from the day before.

I would think it would be very easy to tell.

Of course, this is the same dingbat who told me she didn't like Bam.

"If I can hear him, I won't bring packages to your house," she told me.

"He's in the house when you come, and even if he wasn't, he won't bite you," I assured her.

"He's a German Shepard," she said.

I didn't know what to say to that. *No shit he's a German Shepard, and you're an idiot. What's your point?*

"Yeah, he's a German Shepard, just like the German Shepherds that save you from mailing bombs."

"I don't like dogs. They freak me out."

Okay, so now we have a situation.

She doesn't like dogs, which means I hate her. I wanted to drag her in the house and let Bam lick her to death. Who in the hell hates dogs?

Since dogs freaked her out, I decided to freak her out.

"You know, we have two dogs, not just the German Shepard," I told her. "It's the other one that bites, and she's always running around loose."

I wasn't just screwing with her either. Molly, all eleven pounds of her, will absolutely bite you if she thinks you're a bitch, which means our mail carrier should watch her ass.

I wasn't going to mess with this woman too much. You've gotta be careful with postal workers. They don't shoot up their workplaces like they did in the 90s, but it's still a bad idea to piss them off. A mailperson with a grudge could destroy your life. Think about it.

So now I'm driving around with Lisa's outgoing mail, slowing down at every side street, looking for a slot – any slot – to shove the letter into.

I slammed on my brakes for a few recycling containers, which are the exact size and color as a postal drop box. At one point, I thought about throwing her letter in one of those. If it had been something unimportant, like a thank you letter or a birthday card, I might have done it.

It was a bill, so I continued to look.

There was a mail truck on a side street, and I followed it for a few hundred yards thinking I could run up and give it to him. He was too quick. He'd pull up to a mailbox, slip the mail in, and zip off.

He only slowed down once. It was for a mailbox that had its little red flag up. He put mail in, took mail out, and slapped down the little red flag.

Eureka!

I passed the mail truck and drove about ten houses ahead of him, threw Lisa's letter in somebody's else's mailbox and put the red flag up.

I know he saw me do it, but I also knew he took the letter because I watched him.

This is how complicated life is in early sobriety. Still, I was kind of proud of myself. I felt like I had cracked a code, like I was beating the system and sticking it to the man. I felt that way for several minutes, until I drove another mile down the road and saw two big shiny blue postal boxes, one on each side of the street.

THERE'S NOTHING WRONG with being proud of your sobriety, and there's nothing wrong with celebrating it publicly, especially if you think it will help the people you're sharing it with. That's all good.

Then there's what I did one day about six months earlier. Unfortunately, I didn't have a sponsor back then, so I had the worst possible person as an advisor: myself.

I've said plenty of disappointing things over the years, but usually I *say* dumb shit, not *write* it.

Get a load of my public proclamation, on Facebook, just ten days out of rehab:

"Hi everyone, I think this is my first time on Facebook -- the first time sober anyway.

I went away (a few times) to address that problem. Enough time has gone by now... I can finally say I nailed it. Now if I could only find my car..."

First starters, the little thing about the car isn't funny. I'm not saying it's in poor taste. Poor taste would be fine. No, it's just not funny. I don't like the person who wrote that unfunny thing and signed my name to it.

The rest of it, which wasn't *supposed* to be funny, is *very* funny, in the worst possible way. Diving into a pool before realizing it has no water... it's that kind of funny. People say dumb things in early sobriety, but this... "I can finally say I nailed it?"

If another alcoholic or addict said something like that ten days after treatment, I'd go to their house, stuff them in my car and bring them back to rehab. Saying I nailed it after ten days is akin to like this:

JUDGE: *What's the defendant's plea?*

DEFENDANT: *I'm not guilty, your honor. Seriously, I didn't do it.*

JUDGE: *How did this man get in here and why are we wasting time with a trial when he's already said he he's not guilty?*

In AA, they say you shouldn't beat yourself up too much, but it's fun. Besides, "enough time has gone by." I got this!

I try not to think about my first year after rehab because all I can do is wince. I was like a high school freshman trying to fit in with the seniors, leaving a trail of awkward silence wherever I went.

Unfortunately for me, much of it is recorded for posterity.

Ironically, I ended my last book this way:

"It's all stored in a cloud somewhere, waiting to be written into your future."

Yeah, it's stored in clouds... clouds of remote servers that will be accessible to anyone, no matter how many times you try to delete it. (Which is a lot different than the figurative cloud I was referring to in the book.)

Less than a year after rehab, I produced a trail of photos – narrated by me and posted on Facebook -- that started at our house in South Glens Falls and ran up Route 9 to Queensbury.

It would have been okay, even funny, if I had stopped after an hour, but my photo journey dragged on for days, and it's all stored in a cloud somewhere -- a cloud that is Googleable to old friends who may wat to see what I'm up to these days.

What led me down the trail? I used to have a simple answer for questions like that – "I was drunk" – but these days everything needs explaining.

I eat one meal per day: pizza, right before bed. It's a diet regimen that's the exact opposite of what every nutritionist in the world recommends but, for me, pizza isn't food; it's a way of life. I have sauce running through my veins, just waiting to clot and travel to my heart.

Every night, I'd unsheathe the pizza cutter (yes, "unsheathe" is a word), cut my pizza, wash the pizza cutter and set it in the dry rack.

That wasn't good enough for the child safety czar in our house -- my awesome wife -- who would sweep in behind me to secure the weapon.

In the wee hours of the morning, Lisa sheathed the pizza cutter. It made me feel neglectful and negligent, like I'd left a bunch of dirty hypodermic needles on the counter.

I'm a lucky man. For years up at the lake house, I'd get drunk and forget to sheath my pizza cutter. Thank God no one ever broke into the house and got hold of it.

When someone does something that seems silly to me, I don't tell them it's silly. I politely ask them about it, hoping that, as soon as they think about it, they'll realize it's silly. It's one of the few things I do that's mature.

"Honey, can I ask you something?"

"Of course," Lisa said.

"What's up with the stupid suit of armor on the pizza cutter?"

It started out mature, in my head, then it got snotty on the way out of my mouth.

"I don't want them [Michael and Rachel] to slice their fingers off when they reach for something," she'd tell me.

"Baby, you can't cut yourself with this thing."

To make my point, I grabbed the pizza cutter and rolled it up my arm and across my face. I banged my head with it, jammed it in my arm, used it to scratch my back and my butt and then picked my teeth and scraped my tongue with it.

"See, baby, I'm okay!"

Then I threw it back in the drawer.

"Trust me, you're not okay. Give me that thing."

She snatched it out of the drawer, brought it to the sink and started scrubbing it.

"Why are you doing? I cleaned it last night."

She turned and just stared at me... for quite a few seconds.

"What?" I asked.

"Please tell me you were joking when you stuck that back in the drawer."

"I was going to be the next person to use it, so..."

She dried it off, slipped the protective sheath back on and put it in the drawer.

"You're obsessed with this stupid pizza sheath!" I told her.

"Look who's talking."

Most of this is just harmless ball busting. She does it to me too. I'm just not writing about her digs at me because some of them have a sliver of truth, so why would I repeat them?

I'm probably not the first stepfather to mock his wife for coddling her children, but Lisa gave me a lot of material.

Even when Rachel and Michael were twelve and fourteen, Lisa insisted on driving them to school, so they wouldn't get bullied on the bus.

"That makes no sense," I told her. "The kids on the bus are the same kids they're going to see when they walk into the school. It's not like they drop the bullies off somewhere else."

She always brushed off stuff like that the same way.

"Whatever."

"Honey, I love you, but you're running a cream puff factory."

"Honey, I love you too," she said while looking me up and down, "but you need to stop eating the creampuffs."

ONE NIGHT, I HID the sheath under a basket on the window sill – a basket that never gets moved. I assumed the sheath was gone forever.

The next night, it was right back on the pizza cutter. I have no idea how she found it, but now I was ready to play hardball.

The following morning, I took the sheath, covered it in fake blood, threw it in the snow and posted a picture of it on Lisa's Facebook page.

Lisa called as soon as she saw it.

"You've got to be shitting me."

"Surrender," I told her.

"Yeah... no."

It was getting personal. This wasn't about a pizza sheath; it was about... something else, but it wasn't about a pizza sheath.

I took the sheath to the closest cemetery and snapped a picture of it on a tombstone. I sent it to Lisa and called her.

"What do ya gotta say about that?"

"It's time for Dr. Stiller to adjust your meds again. That's what I have to say about that."

As it turned out, she was right. Over the next few months, as my antic fluctuated from funny to scary, he *did* have to adjust them... not once but three times. Add that to the long list of things I don't give a shit about.

The pizza sheath thing went on for a long time – too long, really.

I went back to the cemetery the next day, but this time I brought Michael. I placed it on a gravestone and told Michael to kneel in front of it, like he was praying.

I took a picture and posted it on Lisa's Facebook page.

The next stop was a popular burger joint, Mr. Bill's, where I took a picture of it hanging around the neck of the big Mr. Bill statue.

Down the road, I got pictures of it floating in the center of a giant puddle in front of a church. That's where I ran into a problem.

While I was posting the pictures on Lisa's Facebook page, the sheath floated out to the middle of the puddle, which wasn't really a puddle; it was more of a pond.

I couldn't retrieve it with a long branch I pulled off one of the church's trees, so I pulled up my pants, took off my socks and shoes and waded out there to get it.

As I made my way back, three church ladies were watching me and whispering to each other. I'd have paid good money to hear what they were saying.

As I posted more and more pictures of the sheath on Lisa's page, the comments from her friends started to multiply, but I didn't stop to read what they were saying.

Next, I dangled the sheath from highway reflectors and stood on Route 9 taking pictures of it at different angles – with cars going sixty miles per hour changing lanes to avoid clipping me.

I brought the sheath to a thruway rest stop to get a picture of it hanging from a "Dog Walk Area" sign. I couldn't reach it at first, so I made a pile of frozen snow at the base to stand on.

There was some gum in my car, so I chewed it till it was gummy enough to stick the sheath on the sign.

As I was doing all this, I wondered what I'd do if a State Trooper pulled up and asked me what I was doing. I didn't want to get caught off guard, so I rehearsed what I'd say, and what he'd say.

Sir, what the fuck are you doing?

I'm just playing a little joke on my wife by hanging this pizza sheath on a thruway sign.

Okay, that's what I thought. Have a good day.

Once that chat was over, I'd ask the trooper to hold the sheath in front of his police car, with the lights on maybe. If he said no, I'd say, "I pay your salary," because cops love it when you say that.

I MAY HAVE BEEN FOGGY, confused, shaky, disoriented, delusional and depressed, but I was learning to make the best of it by doing stuff like this. I didn't have to be lucid for this. Plus, I was learning how to do stuff I'd never done before.

The smart phone was still a novelty to me. I couldn't believe it could do so many things, so I was running around town recording and taking pictures of everything from ducks to churches to people picking their noses.

Don't ask me why, but I loved playing head games with the people at Dunkin' Donuts. Whoever was working the drive-thru was an easy target because I can toy with them from the comfort of my car.

One morning, out of pure boredom, I drove up and placed an order using the dorky, nasally voice that I still use when I'm making fun of Michael.

I was recording everything, of course.

"I'll have a plain bagel, lighhhhhtly toasted, with drawwwn butter."

"Drawn butter?"

"Yes, drawwwn butter, please."

"We don't... have that."

Then I went back to my normal voice.

"Fine! I'll just have an extra-large coffee with cream."

When I got to the window, the guy was freaking out, like I was robbing the place.

Maybe he thought the phone I was pointing at him was a pistol. He was leaning out of the window so far, he could have reached through the window and put the coffee in my cup holder.

He begged me to take the coffee and leave.

I tried to give him money, but he wouldn't take it.

"No, no, here's your coffee, here ya go. On the house."

My first thought was that I found a new way to save three dollars a day. If that's all I had to do for a free coffee, I'd do the exact same thing every morning.

I took the coffee and watched the video, which was even funnier on my phone than it was it person. I sent it to Lisa, just so she knew I was safe and having fun. Then I was off to Crandall Park to take pictures of the ducks.

The drawwwn butter thing isn't even funny. The guy freaking out was funny, but I didn't plan that. But, here's the thing: If you record yourself doing a hundred stupid things a day, at least one of the things will be funny enough to watch repeatedly.

Plus, I had that smartphone, which was still an amazing invention to me. I wasn't going to waste its potential by taking selfies and recording dance recitals. Who does that?

To onlookers, I must have looked like a freed prisoner or a dog seeing snow for the first time – rolling in it, licking it, eating it... soaking it up and letting it sink in.

That's how I felt, and I loved it.

THE WHOLE PIZZA SHEATH thing was supposed to be a private joke between me and Lisa, but I still didn't understand how social media worked. I didn't realize that, when I posted something on her page, all three thousand of her friends could see it – and most of them aren't *really* friends.

As usual, I didn't care, but I wasn't sure if Lisa did. When tons of her friends started leaving comments, I called her.

"I didn't know all those people would see this sheath thing. You can delete it all if you want."

"No! Everyone thinks it's hilarious."

I wonder how many people thought I started drinking again, or maybe they thought I replaced alcohol with heroin or angel dust.

That's the part I didn't care about – what other people thought. At some point, though, I felt obligated to explain myself to the small circle of people whose opinion *did* matter to me.

A forty-seven-old running around town snapping pictures of a pizza sheath isn't right. It seems like a red flag. But, I was just doing what they told me to do. I was just trying not to drink. They told me to go to any lengths.

I couldn't have been *too* far off the beam. People were coming out of the woodwork asking me for advice.

Soon after my dangerously boastful promise on Facebook – *"enough time has gone by, I think I nailed it"* – I started getting a steady stream of private messages from old friends and acquaintances.

The general tone was: *Hey, I just wanted to say hi and see what you were up to these days and, by the way, I have a friend who thinks he might have a drinking problem.*

Suddenly, it seemed like everyone I'd ever known was nervous about their drinking. They felt perfectly comfortable outing themselves to me, which means they thought my behavior was so outrageous, anything they admitted to would pale in comparison. They were right.

Most of them got straight to the point:

"How did you know you were an alcoholic?"

Oh, I don't know. I think it occurred to me when I was running away from Rehab Number Six.

Whenever I get that question, I always say the same thing.

"I couldn't stop. That's usually a good indication."

There's more to it than that, of course, but if someone is looking for a one-line answer, I think that's the best one to give them.

My alcoholism was obvious to everyone with eyes and a brain. It was obvious to me. In my opinion, diagnosing yourself requires nothing more than common sense and honesty. If you can't stop, or if it's hard to stop, you're probably an alcoholic.

One guy I used to work with was a little more reluctant when he called.

"Hey John, how've you been?"

It was Dave, who I hadn't heard from since my awkward departure from the Governor's Office ten years earlier.

I knew he wasn't calling to hear how the food was at my last rehab. At work, he was accustomed to dealing with the press daily, so he chose his words carefully.

"Can we please keep this conversation confidential?" he asked.

"Of course."

"Someone insinuated that I have a drinking problem. I want to ensure I respond to them without sounding defensive."

"What happened, you got a DWI?"

Getting a DWI doesn't mean you're an alcoholic; it means you're an idiot. There's a difference, albeit, a slight one.

"Yes, I got a DWI, which I can deal with," he said. "I just want to make sure I'm not, you know, the A-word."

Oh, you are the A-word, Dave, but you're not an alcoholic.

"Do you *think* you have a problem with alcohol?"

"No, I can take it or leave it. You've seen me."

He's right; I've seen him drink. If he's an alcoholic, he's not a very good one. I told him not to worry.

"I wouldn't lose too much sleep over it. Go to an AA meeting and see if you can identify with what they're saying."

"I don't want to go to an AA meeting," he told me.

"Then let me rephrase it for you. After the judge orders you to go to AA meetings -- and he will -- see if you can identify with what they're saying."

You'd be surprised how many people question themselves on this issue. It's always the result of something bad, usually after a DWI arrest. Suddenly, they're wondering if they're an alcoholic.

Judges routinely send them someplace where they're evaluated for alcoholism. No one passes these tests. If they admit they have more than sixteen drinks per week, they're diagnosed as an alcoholic. If they say they rarely drink, they're diagnosed as a *lying* alcoholic. Naturally, people freak out. Then they call someone they know who's had a problem with booze, like me.

It's a peculiar thing, people coming to me for advice about their drinking. Wouldn't I be the last person to ask? It's like going to Bill Cosby for advice on how to treat women.

I'll never refuse to help someone who's struggling. I'll do whatever I can. In the future, I should start with a warning that doing it my way increases the odds that you'll die.

I could do it with a recording, just like they do in those prescription drug commercials where the disclaimer takes up ninety percent of the commercial.

"You're seeking guidance from someone who drank every day for fifteen years before going to his first rehab. He stayed sober for three months, then overdosed on Klonopin. He drank for another ten years, then flunked out of six rehabs before completing one – for a grand tally of seven rehabs and twenty-five years of heavy drinking."

Then I could ask them if they still want my guidance.

Clearly, I don't know how to get sober. Still, people always ask, "How did you do it?"

I didn't do it. They shoved me into a car and took me to the hospital. The only reason I didn't run was because I was too weak to fight anymore. That's the extent of me doing anything. Ask my mother. Ask my wife. Ask my aunt. Hell, ask Bam. He was there. Not only was he there, he helped usher my drunk ass out the door.

For years, he stood at the front door, protecting me from anyone who came within fifty feet of the house.

I knew a lot of people in town who had police scanners. They'd tell me that the police were always talking to each other about Bam, saying he was making it impossible to get anywhere near the house.

Towards the end, when I was in rough shape, I used to pass out on the living room floor, and when I woke up, Bam would be lying next to me, licking my face.

The last time the police showed up with an ambulance crew, Bam didn't even bark. In fact, someone later told me it looked like Bam was relieved they were there, that he was waving them in the door.

I never quit drinking; drinking quit me. After twenty-five years of committed, faithful daily drinking, alcohol just suddenly stopped working. Even if I guzzled vodka, which isn't recommended, I couldn't get drunk. At best, it would take away my withdrawal symptoms, like shaking. Then after a while, it stopped doing even that.

How's that for a quandary? Drinking alcohol wasn't taking away my alcohol withdrawal symptoms. But – and this is a big but – I still had to drink all day and all night, or else my withdrawal symptoms would be unbearable, even deadly.

It was the ultimate betrayal. Alcohol turned on me after I devoted my life to it. It's like falling in love with someone and agreeing to spend the rest of your life on a deserted island with them, then getting there and finding out they have smallpox.

I was dying of thirst and drinking water didn't help. It's not a good place to be.

DAVE WASN'T DONE with me yet. He got the answer he was hoping for – *"Don't worry, you're not an alcoholic"* -- so now he felt compelled to return the favor by asking a few questions about me.

"Have you been writing much?"

"Notes to my wife… an occasional email."

"That's it? Why?" He asked.

"When I clear up a bit more, I'm thinking about writing a book about alcoholism," I said. "Please don't tell anyone, though."

"Who am I gonna tell?"

Why do people say that when you ask them not to tell anyone?

Who are you going to tell? I have no fucking idea who you might tell. I'm telling you to keep your mouth shut around everyone.

Add that to my phone directory of pet peeves.

I don't know why I told him I was writing a book. I wasn't.

I thought my overdose and subsequent alcohol abuse killed my writing career. It *did* kill my writing career. After the Governor's Office, I took a job repairing arcade games and managing a paintball shooting gallery. Then I worked in a zoning office.

The only writing I did after the Governor's Office was in 2010. After not writing a thing for three years, I wrote and published a myriad of op-ed pieces in 2010, including one in the *New York Times* – a newspaper I can't stand.

I tried figuring the whole thing out when I found the newspaper clippings a year after leaving rehab. It was creepy. On *Law and Order*, serial killers and stalkers always tape newspaper clippings about their crimes on the wall.

I didn't go that far – mine were stuffed in a box -- but it was clear that the seclusion at the lake house had gotten to me because it looked like I wrote them out of paranoia.

The articles weren't about issues I cared about. The one in the *Times* was about the redevelopment of Lower Manhattan. Another one was about the fracking.

They weren't written in my voice. They were more academic than conversational. It just didn't make any sense. They weren't related to anything important or pressing, but I wrote all of them – about twenty of them -- in the span of less than two weeks.

That's fast for me... like I was working on a deadline.

Why the mad rush to get these articles into newspapers so quickly, only to disappear into my cave again after they were published? I must have had a good reason.

I used to worry that a white van was going to show up to the lake house and take me somewhere. My plan was always to open fire on anyone who came to the house wearing a white uniform, especially if they were holding a big butterfly net.

Maybe I thought that writing these articles would convince people that I was smart and sane. Who knows.

For the first eleven months of sobriety, I had the same thoughts. I was having delusions, and I *knew* they were delusions but not until after I acted on them. By then, the damage was already done.

I wasn't watching out for the big white van anymore, but I was worried that sobriety was making it hard to hide a mental illness.

Things started to change just in time.

I'd all but ignored the readings of Alcoholics Anonymous, including this Pollyannaish promise about the rewards of the program: "Our Whole Attitude and Outlook Upon Life Will Change."

They read that line, as part of the Twelve Promises of AA, at the end of every meeting. It's what I was hoping for – a new outlook on life -- but, after ten months, I wasn't seeing any signs that I would get it.

If I thought I'd be permanently stuck in the fog of post-alcohol-whatever, there wouldn't be much of a reason to stay sober. The AA literature *promised* I would clear up, but it didn't say when.

I *knew* getting drunk would clear me up because that's what my brain and body were accustomed to. It was tempting. I was getting tired of being a zombie.

Stiller said it would take a year for me to clear up, and that's the only promise I was banking on.

After eleven months of weird highs and depressing lows, I got what I'd been waiting for.

Chapter Seven

And This is My Brain on Pizza

ONE YEAR SOBER

I never expected a sudden day of clarity. I never thought the cloud would just vanish all at once. All along, I thought things would clear up gradually, getting a little better each day.

It didn't happen that way. The problem got worse before it disappeared. For about a half hour, the cloud that I'd been walking through for nearly a year got thicker and darker. I was more confused than ever -- dizzy, disoriented and panic-stricken. Then it just ended. I just walked right out of it while feeding the ducks at Crandall Park. Maybe it was the quacking.

Just like that – in less than an hour -- I felt better than I'd felt in years, maybe decades.

The one thing I'll always remember most is the way the top of the pine trees looked against the backdrop of the sky. It felt like I could see every branch and every needle as if they were hanging right in front of me.

Everything – the trees, the sky and the ducks -- were sharper and more colorful than ever. I was alert, and totally aware of everything around me. And for the rest of that day and ever since, I no longer felt sick and tired.

Was it a miracle? Probably not. There were no fig trees or dancing lepers or wine... definitely no wine.

At the time, I assumed my incredible experience was the long-term effects of alcohol dissipating into the thin, bluer-than-ever air. Still, it felt better than my finest buzz from alcohol, and that's about the closest thing to a miracle I'll experience in my lifetime.

If it was a miracle, Dr. Stiller is God because he told me when it would happen. His prognosis was right on the mark. My day of clarity came almost one year after I left rehab.

That's when I when I decided to write, *You Can't Die: A Day of Clarity*. It suddenly made sense. I had just emerged from a long twenty-five year nightmare. Probably for the rest of my life, I would be looking back on it and asking myself, "What in the hell happened?"

I wrote the first book – and this one -- to provide my best guess at an answer, an answer that had the potential for a happy ending.

There was another reason for the book, a reason manifest in a text I got from Jackson not long ago.

"Last night," he told me, "I had a dream that you were addicted to crystal meth."

The good news is that my kids are thinking about me at night. The bad news is obvious.

People have dreams based on thoughts and ideas that are already floating around in their head. I've never even seen crystal meth, but after all the time I spent in hospitals and rehabs, what did I expect to be floating around in Jackson's head?

Here's my thinking on that. If I never had a drinking problem, Jackson's bad dreams about me would be based on other things, like my writing or even my wrestling.

Last night, I had a dream that your job was giving foot massages to good writers.

Last night, I had a dream that you wrestled Matt Lauer in the finals of a big tournament and he was disqualified for ejaculating on your back.

These are bad dreams, but they're still better than the prospect of me smoking crystal meth or drinking again. I'd take the Matt Lauer thing over getting drunk again, any day.

With almost a year of sobriety under my belt, I was finally starting to believe that I would – that I could – live the rest of my life without drinking again.

For the next few weeks, I wandered around Glens Falls enjoying the clarity, the steadiness of hand and the general feeling of being healthy, something I hadn't felt in decades.

As the days and weeks went on, I noticed other changes in my daily life. I wasn't sweating for no reason, and my stutter was gone.

I still had an occasional "drunk dream," but I wasn't having them every night, and when I woke up, I knew it was just a dream... that I didn't really relapse.

I still had highs and lows, but the lows weren't so debilitatingly low anymore.

The brain I was born with was functioning the way it did before I started drinking heavily in my twenties. But no one ever promised me that my brain was normal to begin with, and it wasn't.

I wasn't sure what the doctors at the Caron Foundation were trying to tell me in the Spring of 2013. I had been threatening to leave if they didn't give me a higher dose of Librium to help me through withdrawal from alcohol.

Instead of giving it to me, they called me into an office and showed me two colorful x-ray images.

There were two doctors in there with me. One was an asshole... and so was the other one. The bigger asshole pointed to one of the images and looked at me very seriously.

"This is your brain."

I was waiting for the other doctor to crack an egg and say, "And this is your brain on drugs."

He pointed to the other image and said, "This is a normal brain."

I was trying to figure out how and where they got a picture of my brain. I don't remember posing for it.

"That's interesting," I said. "Can we talk about Librium?"

We talked about it. They told me to go fuck myself. I'm paraphrasing.

The only thing I remember about the brain images they showed me is that one was yellowish with a big rounded X in the center. The other one looked like a pizza with a clump of cheese in the middle.

My brain was the pizza, which makes perfect sense since that's all I eat. I later learned that they didn't have an actual scan of my brain. They were showing me a brain scan that was consistent with the information in my medical file.

I had a brain scan done in 2003, after my overdose, but these wingnuts didn't have it. So whatever information they had about me couldn't have been very flattering.

I'm aware that, somewhere in my vast, mysterious medical file, there's a mental illness diagnosis. That doesn't bother me. For starters, I faked a mental illness three times to get into a comfortable mental health unit instead of a rehab. I knew what I was doing. I knew my way around the flight deck.

Even if there is a brain scan that indicates my pizza is a little saucy, who cares? Saucy compared to who, everyone else? I never wanted to be like everyone else. Maybe the problem isn't with me. Maybe it's everyone else.

As it turned out, being like everyone else wasn't even in the cards. But, a year after rehab, I felt good, very good. More importantly, I felt like the same person all day. The mood spikes, the impulsiveness, the violent tendencies and the highs and lows... all that crap was gone. There was no longer a need to drink.

I DIDN'T TELL ANYONE in AA that it was my one-year anniversary of being sober. They like to celebrate that stuff with cake and coins and cards, and that's just not my style. Despite my improved state, I wasn't looking for that much attention.

In AA, they talk about rejoining society and "getting back into life." Now, it was October of 2014, exactly one year after leaving treatment, and I was looking forward to getting back into life by participating in Halloween for the time since I was twelve.

Yeah, I know, but... baby steps.

I don't remember what I wore the last time I trick or treated in the late 70s. I'm positive it was something half-assed. I may have scribbled red marker on my face and said I was a murdered child. Or maybe I rubbed dirt on my knees and said I was a baseball player.

The point was to get as much candy possible with the least effort.

Somewhere along the line, Halloween changed – a lot.

By 2014, Halloween, as I remember it, was gone, replaced with good behavior, paranoid parents, safe neighborhoods and a ton of political correctness.

Now that I was sober and paying attention again, I was shocked when I learned the new rules.

What ever happened to "Devil's Night"?

And when did clowns became the enemy? Stick a red rubber nose on your face these days, and half the neighborhood calls 911 and the other half loads its shotguns.

If Ronald McDonald is a pedophile, what's the burglar being charged with? He was a crook already. How is McDonalds still in business?

Sorry, but Halloween isn't Halloween without Trick-or-Treating, and Trick-or-Treating isn't Trick-or-Treating without the Trick.

Instead of Trick-or-Treating, they should call it Molly-and-Coddling, and instead of Halloween, they should call it stupid.

Where's the fun in eating bags of candy if you don't run the risk of biting into a razor blade or a funny-colored pill? What ever happened to the glorious tradition of eating a Snickers Bar, then having to pick pins and needles out of your tongue?

Where's the honor in making it around the block if you don't run the risk of someone beating you up and taking your candy?

And where are all the smashed pumpkins?

The last time I was sober, there were more pumpkins on the streets than there were on doorsteps. We used to smash people's pumpkins and throw the pieces at cars.

People put their pumpkins on their doorsteps *expecting* them to get smashed. That's where the band "Smashing Pumpkins" got their name.

I didn't know about the clown stigma until a year after I got out of rehab. Mallory sent me a text, apparently thinking I'd know better than to listen to her.

"Dad, I need a video of you running around outside dressed like a clown. Can you do that?"

She was expecting me to laugh and tell her to go... wherever.

"Um, okay. I won't even ask why," I told her.

"Oh, and I need it in the next couple hours."

At this point, she was still joking, but I didn't know it at the time.

I hauled ass to CVS, Walgreens and Rite Aid. None of them had clown masks. I didn't know why. It's a good thing I didn't ask. The cops would have shown up and given me a baton beatdown in the parking lot.

I finally gave up and bought a ton of make-up and a monster mask that had clowny hair, then flew back to the house to find Rachel.

"I need you to put this makeup on the mask. I want it to look like a clown."

"Why didn't you just buy a clown mask?" Rachel asked.

"I couldn't find one anywhere."

She laughed.

"Probably because everyone wants to kill them," she said.

I had no idea what that meant, but that was generally the case when Rachel spoke to me, so I didn't bother to ask.

She held the mask in one hand and the makeup in the other and stared down at them, looking confused.

"So... what's the mask for? Why don't I just put the makeup on your face."

Hmm. Okay, she's right for once.

I had to save face, so to speak. I didn't want to admit I was an idiot, so I made something up.

I did the thing where I use seemingly-relevant words, out of order, in a long sentence.

"It's gotta be over the hair rubber in the nose back to the skin because the ears and clowns, don't have time, hurry up."

As usual, the mumbo jumbo tactic did the trick, and she started my transformation.

A half hour later, I was a full-blown clown, and Rachel was recording me running through the woods behind the house, hiding behind trees and jumping out of the tool shed.

We wound up with some solid, action-packed footage.

I sent it to Mallory and waited anxiously by the phone to hear her reaction.

She texted back a few minutes later.

"Oh, sorry. I don't need it anymore. It's pretty funny though."

Excuse me? Pretend I'm your father and say that again.

"What did you want it for?"

"I was going to post it on YouTube. I thought it'd be funny because of everything that's going on with clowns, but I didn't want you to get shot."

It's just what every daddy wants to hear from his little girl, that she didn't want to get him capped.

A few days later, it was Halloween, and I still didn't have a costume to wear while passing out candy at the door.

I had a creepy mask, the one worn by "Anonymous." By itself, it wasn't scary enough. I needed something so terrifying that all the neighbors would be talking about it the next day.

After thinking about it all morning, I decided to make a scary sign.

In big black letters, the sign said, "Everyone Dies."

Hear me out.

Kids think death is just something that happens to their grandparents. My sign was scary because, you know, it reminded them how life really works: first grandpa, then you.

I couldn't wait to show Lisa. I got dressed up, grabbed my sign and struck my pose.

"Honey, come in here."

She was saying something to Michael as she walked into the room. It was funny to hear the tone of her voice change mid-sentence, the second she saw me.

"I need to go pick up Rachel and... *what the hell is wrong with you?*"

"You think it's scary?"

"Clowns and death? How about something that won't get you arrested," she said.

"It's not a clown. It's the 'Anonymous' dude."

I threw out another idea, one I knew she'd hate, just to make the death sign seem like the better alternative.

"How about making me up to look like the ex-smokers on commercials -- with half a face, one brown tooth and a nasty bent cigarette hanging out of my mouth. The kids with parents who smoke will run away crying, thinking their parents are going to die."

"Yeah, I'll hand out the candy," she said.

"Darn. Well, okay."

Of course, that was my objective all along.

Now that I got out of door duty, all I had to do is run to the store and get the candy.

I hear people say life is simpler in sobriety. It's *better*, but I learned early on in sobriety to kiss the simplest things in life goodbye, like buying Halloween candy.

For a long time, the only checking out I did was at the liquor store in Chestertown and the mini-mart four hundred yards down the road.

When I was drinking, my hand was too shaky to sign the credit card slip. The cashier in Chestertown always signed it for me.

I'd go into the store, grab a thirty-pack and walk out. They had my credit card, so I never even stopped at the counter. The whole transaction required two words from me: "Hey" on the way in, and "Thanks" on the way out.

Compare that to buying Halloween candy at Rite Aid.

If I had known what was waiting for me in there, I would have dressed up like Little Miss Muffet and cheerfully handed out candy at the door.

I had an uncomfortable feeling when I walked up to the counter.

The checkout lady's official Rite Aid shirt was a like billboard for charitable causes. She had a different color ribbon for every form of cancer ever detected in a lab rat.

From collar to belt, she was plastered with stickers and buttons and pins promoting everything from discount offers to flu shot reminders.

As I plopped down my bags of candy, I got the impression we were going to discuss more than money and my Kit Kat bars.

"Hi, I just have these," I said.

"Do you have your Plenti card?"

"Yep, right here."

"Do you want to sign up for the Wellness Rewards Program?"

"No, I'm doing fine without that."

"We have free flu shots in the pharmacy. Have you had yours yet?"

"Yeah, I did." *I had a vasectomy too. Want me to prove it?*

I could hear bags crumpling behind me. People were lining up.

"Would you like to donate a dollar to the Children's Miracle Network?"

"Okay." *The real miracle will be if the children get any of it.*

"And did you want to leave your change for the Kids Cents program?"

"Yes... yep." *No, lady, I want the people behind me to think I'm a cheap, heartless prick. How about I just leave my wallet here, so I can get home before this candy expires.*

"Okay, hold on a minute while I print out your coupons."

Got any coupons for beer? At this point, I'd like to get drunk.

I guarantee the people behind me were contemplating how they were going to answer all the same questions.

Since I said yes to everything, now they had to. I wanted to turn around and tell them, "Give her fifty bucks right off the bat, just to keep the line moving."

That story makes me sound like a miserable jerk, and I didn't quit drinking to be one of those. Some people think I'm cynical. No, I'm sarcastic. There's a difference.

How can I be cynical? Somewhere in that marathon transaction, I donated money to cancer research, even though they haven't made a gnat's testicle of progress in treating cancer in two hundred years.

They're still trying to hack cancer out of our bodies with machetes. If that doesn't work, they make us lay down while they walk into a safe room where they press a button to nuke our breasts and prostates. What are cancer researchers doing, other than killing lab rats?

Cancer research -- give me a break. If cancer researchers made half as much progress over the past century as Silicon Valley geeks have made with phones, there wouldn't be any cancer and everyone would be running around smoking, snorting red meat and using their sunscreen lotion for more enjoyable things.

That's probably why the government doesn't want a cure for cancer.

See? I'm not cynical.

The point of recovery is to become a better person, not an angry one. I surround myself with people who lift me up, especially the ones who fell as far down the scale as I did. No one is happier to be alive than those of us who hit rock bottom and found their way back up.

I know a few people who quit drinking, then came into AA and blamed everyone else for their problems... and wound up drinking again.

Every night, I want to pray for those people. I've never done it, but I want to.

Chapter Eight

Juan and the Killer Turkeys

ONE YEAR, FIVE MONTHS SOBER

Juan was concerned about rednecks in Chestertown. We were on our way up there from Glens Falls, which has its own fair share of rednecks, so Juan could see the lake house I was always talking about in meetings.

"Those good ole boys will take one look at me and round up a posse."

"It's Loon Lake, not Selma," I told him.

"How many black people are up there?"

"None," I said. "Which means nothing and, by the way, you're not black."

"Okay, then how many Puerta Ricans are there?"

"I don't sit around counting people," I said. "But none."

"What about bears?"

"The bears are black," I said.

And that's the only thing that's black in Chestertown. In fact, the school district's last statistics on race didn't even include charts and graphs and numbers. It just said, "We're all white."

One year, the racial numbers went up slightly, but that was the year Charles, who's black, stood up as best man in my wedding. District officials tried to count that.

None of the above reflects anything sinister or racist. The demographics don't shift very often in the Adirondacks. Extended families tend to stick around, from birth to death. Outsiders come to visit, not live. There's not a lot of people moving there on purpose. It aint Silicon Valley.

We got off the Adirondack Northway and drove about fifty yards into Chestertown when Juan had his first girly moment.

"What the hell is that?"

"It's a wild turkey. Settle down."

"What about all that?" he yelled, pointing at a flock of turkeys further down the road.

As we drove on, even I was shocked. There were turkeys everywhere – on the side of the road, in the middle of the road, and pouring out of the woods like they were being chased by bears.

That would have really freaked Juan out.

I've never seen so many damn turkeys in my life, in Chestertown or anywhere else. Occasionally, I've seen one or two of them wandering around behind the lake house, but I didn't even know this many turkeys existed.

I pretended not to be surprised because I wanted Juan's Deliverance concept of the Adirondacks to be even more fucked up than it already was. That way, I could really screw with him when we got to the lake.

"There must be something going on," Juan said. "That's a lot of turkeys."

"I guarantee there's a redneck with a shotgun behind every one of them," I told him.

Juan is a reformed street thug from Springfield. I'm not being mean. That's how he describes himself because that's what he was.

On paper, Juan and I have a lot in common. Technically, we have the same name, since Juan is the Spanish form of John. We're only a matter of hours apart in age. He was born just five days before me in November of 1965. And we both did hard time in the armpit of America -- Springfield, Massachusetts.

When I was at Springfield College – drinking, wrestling, and occasionally going to classes -- Juan was on the other side of town –drinking, selling crack and occasionally going to prison.

If only I'd known, we could have done lunch.

He wasn't selling *real* crack; he was selling little chucks of Ivory soap that *looked* like crack.

Juan was worse than a drug dealer; he used to rob drug dealers. He'd steal anything. One time, he stole a guy's car battery, then sold it back to the same guy the next day.

He was arrested more than twenty times and spent nine years in prison.

I hated punks like Juan. If you told me about Juan ten years ago and asked me if I could ever be in the same room with him, I'd say, "Only to watch his execution."

And yet, after decades of trusting no one except Charles, Juan was the first person in AA that I trusted enough to bring to the lake house. The only reason I never go inside his house is because I'm afraid of his girlfriend.

For a while, people in AA quietly suspected me and Juan of being lovers. They said it jokingly, but I can always tell when someone is half joking and half asking.

It's not true. I swear, even if I were gay, I wouldn't get nasty with Juan. I don't think he could shut up long enough to do the one thing I'd want Juan to do if I were gay.

Plus, I'd probably want a fella with a nice head of flowing hair. Who wants to look down at Juan's shiny head?

One day, we were at Target picking up supplies for an AA anniversary celebration. We'd just come from the gym, so we were in tank tops and shorts.

After picking out cookies and cake, we were in the greeting card section when Juan's mood suddenly changed. It happens.

"Let's get out of here."

"Why?"

"People think we're together," he said.

"We are together," I said.

"No, I mean *together* together. They think you're my bitch."

"I'm *your* bitch? Where do you get that?"

He looked me up and down, like I really was his bitch.

"You're the one carrying *my* cake and cookies."

I could have reminded Juan that the only bitch in his life was waiting for him at home. Again, I'm not being mean; I'm just repeating what he's constantly telling me. Granted, he didn't know I'd be writing about it.

Juan has been begging for this abuse. I will never get back the gazillions of hours I spent listening to him vent about his woman or girlfriend or fiancé or wife or crazy bitch, depending on Juan's mood and the day of week. Most days, it's crazy bitch.

That's why this book doesn't have an index. If someone is curious enough to see if they got dissed, they'll have to read the whole thing.

One time, Juan started griping about her as soon as we got in the car on Maple Street in Glens Falls. He continued to rant all the way to the Aviation Mall in Queensbury.

Note the irony: That's the exact route I drove while in the funeral procession -- from St. Michaels to a hole in the ground at the cemetery, which is exactly where she's driving him.

Finally, Juan decided to stop ranting and take a breath, so I seized the opportunity to speak.

"This is the kind of conversation I try to avoid."

"What kind?"

"The kind where you're talking and I'm listening."

THE LAKE HOUSE WAS BEING renovated, which is why we were there in the first place, but none of the renovation guys were at the house.

A note was taped to the wall. It was from O'Malley, the floor guy who I've known for years. It said, "We need to talk."

That's kind of a stern note to get from your floor guy. What could be so serious? The grout doesn't match the window treatments?

I flashed the note at Juan.

"Sounds like he's breaking up with you," he said.

"Maybe he found out about us."

As instructed, I called O'Malley.

He told me that some pipes under the floor needed to be rerouted before he could finish one of the bathrooms. It seemed to me he could have put that information in his bitchy note. Perhaps he thought it would be ill-mannered to break the news to me that way.

There had to be more. There's always more.

"I called Jeremy at ADK Plumbers," O'Malley said. "He doesn't want to do any work at *your* house. Is there something you forgot to tell me?" His tone was stanky-like, and he put extra stank on "your."

"Why?"

"You tell me."

Now I was getting a little pissed, and Juan knew it. If I didn't know any better, I'd think O'Malley was the boss in this relationship.

"I don't even know the guy," I said.

"He knows you."

I knew where this was heading. He knew me, but I didn't know him. If I had a dollar, etcetera.

Obviously, I did something really fucked up to him when I was drinking. I'd been having conversations like this at least once a week since I got out of rehab.

Here's my policy on stuff I may or may not have done when I was drinking: I'm willing to apologize for stuff I don't remember. It would be nice if the incident rang a bell, but it's not mandatory.

But O'Malley wanted to tease me with third party guessing games. I don't do that.

I had no problem apologizing to this plumber, whoever he was, but first I needed O'Malley to spit it the fuck out. I wasn't going to let the floor guy scold me like I was a naughty kindergartner.

You know what you did young man!

"Call me back when you know what you want to say," I told him, and I was about to hang up when more words came out of his mouth.

"It had something to do with your dog, and you told him to go fuck himself. I told him you were probably drunk."

Now *that* rang a bell. It was precisely the kind of interaction I had with people in my drinking days.

O'Malley was wrong about one thing. I probably wasn't drunk. Sober alcoholics can be ornery and violent, none more so than me. Apparently, an Adirondack plumber can testify to that. In court, a lot of people *did* testify to that.

Sober alcoholics are like drunk wolverines: nasty as fuck.

As a kid, I used to hide in the backyard when my dad was sober. He was scary when he was sober. Then he'd have a few Genesee Cream Ales, which is also scary -- and, suddenly, it was safe to be around him. As a kid, how could I not be left with the impression that beer was a good thing? I didn't even drink it and I needed it in my life.

When it comes to apologizing for things that allegedly happened, I have no way of knowing what's true and what's someone else's version of true. Thing is, I can remember certain days and conversations right down to the smallest detail, but I don't remember anything at all about other things... like 1999, 2006, 2009 and 2010.

Oddly, I can remember virtually everything that happened from 2011 to 2013, when I was under the influence of alcohol every minute of every day.

O'MALLEY PATCHED THINGS up with the plumber and the plumber patched things up with the floor and everyone was happy... except Juan.

"Where's the damn lake?"

117

"Oh, yeah. That is why we came up here, isn't it?"

"Yeah. I wanna see a lake."

"Did you say *the* lake or *a* lake?" I asked.

"*A* lake. I've never been to one," he said.

I pointed to the lake.

"It's right there."

Juan didn't just walk to the beach; he gravitated there, like earthlings being drawn in by an alien spaceship. He didn't say a word; he was just taking it all in.

We walked out on my dock. The water was like glass. It must have been surreal for someone experiencing the serenity of a lake for the first time.

I wondered what had him in awe, the sheer size of the lake or the serenity. I was dying to hear what he had to say.

"You know what else that bitch did?"

And he was off to the races again.

WE HUNG OUT ON a picnic table for a while, talking mostly about Juan's, umm, challenging relationship and how to get out of it. I had, like, three hundred ideas.

Out of the corner of my eye, I could see movement on the adjoining beach.

"Who's that?" Juan asked.

He was pointing toward a dark-skinned family on the adjoining beach. They recently purchased a lake house that shares the beach next to ours.

"Oh, that's right." I said. "There *are* Puerta Ricans in Chestertown."

"They're Dominican."

"How in the hell can you tell that from a hundred feet away?" I asked.

"Can you tell if a dude is white from a hundred feet?"

"Yeah," I said, "but I can't tell if he's Irish or Scottish."

That's the way it is with me and Juan... back and forth all day. It's the kind of thing that makes my life worth living.

We spent a lot of time talking about Springfield that day, mostly about how much we hated it. I don't know who hates it more, him or me. I guess it depends on whether there's a statute of limitations on bench warrants. If there's not, I hate it more and I'm never going back there. His mother still lives in Springfield, so he goes back three or four times a year.

There's only one way I can safely go back: Via satellite. Later that night, that's what I did, using one of my favorite things online or off – Google Earth.

What I stumbled on that night inspired me to write "Life with Eric and Andy," which became Chapter Two of *You Can't Die: A Day of Clarity*...

Chapter Nine

Andy from Above

ALMOST TWO YEARS SOBER

Since the events in that chapter took place more than twenty-five years earlier, I had to go searching for certain details. Fortunately, a lot of the details were still pickling in the mysterious swamp that is Eric Jackson's brain.

A couple people questioned me about that. Specifically, they were "curious" about my ability to reconstruct old events and conversations.

One person skeptically called it my "remarkable knack for recalling drunken memories." The first thing I told this person is what I always tell people who talk to me that way: *Bite me.*

It was a fair question, though. Some of the details were fresh in my brain because I told the story a million times over the years. Eric Jackson filled in the blanks.

In other cases, I had to go back, interview old friends or family members. I pored over old emails, phone records, writings, speeches and even billing statements.

I even managed to retrieve old voicemails. They were from late 2012 and early 2013, which was when I was at rock bottom. Listening to the messages brought me right back there.

Of the twenty messages in the mailbox, eight were from my mother, five were from Lisa, one was from Jackson and six were from people who are as irrelevant to this book as they were in my life.

Lisa's message sounded desperate.

"Honey, you don't have to talk if you don't want to, but just let me know you're there and you're alright."

Jackson sounded like a little boy.

"Uh hey dad, I'm just calling to say hi."

I could hear the anxiety in his voice.

And then there was mom.

"John... John... pick up. It's mom, call me back."

Just for fun, I returned the call.

"Hey, mom. I'm just calling you back. What's up?"

"Oh, did I call you?" she asked.

"Yeah, four years ago. Sorry it took me so long to get back to you. What did you want?"

The absurdity of me finding, then returning, a message from three years ago flew right past her.

"Oh. So, what are you up to?"

USING GOOGLE EARTH, I was able to return to the scene of certain crimes.

I zoomed in on Andy's house in Springfield, where Eric and I lived during our senior year in college. I was trying to resurrect details of several incidences that took place in 1987, including a car accident I got into on New Year's Eve.

I was dating a dancer named Desiree, who lived with another dancer named Athena. By nine o'clock, all three of us were drunk. I was, by far and as usual, the drunkest. Right after the ball dropped, they decided to ring in the New Year by attacking me… in a good way.

If ever there was an incident whose details I wish I could recall, it was this one. I'd even settle for being able to zoom in on it with Google Earth thirty years later. What I do remember is that Desiree disapproved of the attention I was giving Athena.

The quality of the attention I was giving Athena couldn't have been very good. In fact, as I recall, the two of them rolled away to do their own thing and I was just an onlooker. Either way, the three-way fantasy quickly turned into a three-way fight and I left.

I don't remember driving home, but I know I did because I sideswiped several parked cars on State Street, which is around the corner from Andy's street.

The next morning, Andy said something about the new paint job on my car. I ran out to the driveway. My cream-colored Cutlass Supreme had horizontal streak marks, in a variety of colors, running from bumper to bumper.

I walked down the street to see what I had done. There were three cars with damage and they matched the three colors on my car.

I went back to Andy's and crammed the Cutlass into a small space behind the house. Then I used Compound White and Andy's belt sander to remove the streaks of paint.

That's right; after three years of college, I used a belt sander to clean my car.

Later that day, I was sitting in Andy's living room with a case of Milwaukee's Best. They say sex is like pizza because, even when it's bad, it's still pretty good. That's kind of true when it comes to pizza but, in my experience, it's not even close to being true about sex.

It's mostly true with beer. Brands like Milwaukee's Best, Piels and Keystone... all of them will get you drunk, but it's a cheap, white trash kind of drunk -- the kind of drunk that makes you want to watch Jerry Springer and Mama June.

It also makes you forget stuff, so I don't remember exactly how it all went down. Apparently, one of Andy's neighbors called the police the morning after the accident. He'd seen the damaged cars on State Street, then he saw me covering up the evidence on my car.

There's no way he could have made the connection with just those two pieces of evidence. He must have seen something else the night before while he was out trolling for underage hookers.

The police came; I remember that. I didn't get arrested. Obviously, I remember that. I just don't remember how I squirmed out of the whole mess.

At my wedding reception two years later, in 1989, Andy mentioned the incident. He said the real trouble started when I found out the neighbor called the police an hour before they rolled up to the house.

Since the guy was notoriously anal about the upkeep of his lawn, I retaliated by throwing sticks in his yard.

I swear to God, every time I think of my obnoxious, twenty-one-year-old-self doing that, I laugh my ass off. What a prick I was.

According to Andy, when the police showed up, I told them I had been waxing and removing rust from my car and the only reason I threw sticks in the guy's lawn was because he wouldn't stop staring at me.

The police didn't think the sticks were enough to warrant an arrest. Andy said my defense was that sticks aren't really litter because they're part of nature.

"You kept telling the cops, *'I was just moving nature, I was just moving nature.'*"

They apparently ordered me to go over to the guy's yard and pick the nature up. According to Andy, I didn't even have to do that much because the guy didn't want "that gorilla stepping on my grass."

Now, thirty years later, I was hovering over the scene of the crime with Google Earth grinning and shaking my head in disbelieve that, after all these years, I haven't evolved as a walking creature one bit.

I was hoping something would jog my memory about how I swerved into a row of parked cars on State Street, even though it's obvious. I was drunk. It was a little late to blame it on a squirrel, and if a guy walked out in front of me that night, he was probably gone by now.

Maybe I swerved to avoid hitting Juan while he was jacking a car battery.

I took a virtual walk down the street where the cars were parked, then continued virtual walking all the way back to Andy's house where I hid my car.

I looked at the neighbor's house. As I was doing all of this, I felt like I died and now I was standing with God, looking down at my life of sinful behavior.

This was just one of the many incidents I left out of the first book for one reason or another. I was advised to not write about anything that could still have an unexpired statute of limitations.

I ignored a bench warrant for assault in 1988. Bench warrants never expire so I'll just put a period on that story right here.

The statute of limitations ran out on the hit and run two decades ago, but I didn't want to test my luck by mentioning either incident in the first book.

Of course, the Ninth Step of Alcoholics Anonymous is all about making amends.

So, if your 1970s or 1980s vehicle was parked on State Street one summer night in 1988, sorry about that. Send me a picture of the damage, and I'll head over there with Compound White and Andy's sander.

I should have gone to jail. If I had, maybe Juan and I would have become friends thirty years ago. More likely, he would have shot me, or I would have beaten him to death.

It's funny to think that, if any one of the thousands of experiences in our lives had been slightly different, one or both of us would be dead. I guess it's not that funny.

In the process of nosing around Andy's yard, I saw a motorcycle parked on the side of his house. Andy hated motorcycles. For a hundred reasons, he would never be caught dead on one, mostly because they're impossible to steer with a Quarter-pounder in one hand and a milkshake in the other.

There was also what appeared to be a garden in the backyard. Last I checked, gardens are used for growing healthy food, like vegetables.

Something was off.

I Googled Andy's full name and other key details, thinking he must have moved. I was hoping to find his phone number so I could tell him about all the rehabs I'd been to since we last talked.

Instead, the search led me straight to his obituary. It was a lengthy article, and it mentioned an unexpected death following a two-week illness but gave no details.

I felt guilty, especially because he came to my wedding in 1989 and we lost touch soon after that. He died on March 23, 2007. Eric and I had gone eight years without even knowing he was dead.

I called Eric.

"I've gotta text you something," I told him.

"What?"

"Andy's obituary."

He didn't say a word.

This couldn't be the same Eric who gleefully raced across campus one day to tell me about the death of a guy we used to smoke pot with.

It was in 1986 and I was just returning from summer break when Eric and his evil smirk broke the news to me.

"Hey, you wanna go behind Gulick Hall and get high?" he asked.

"I do."

"Okay, wait here and I'll run upstairs and get Kyle," he said.

He ran about ten feet, then turned around.

"Oh wait, we can't get high with Kyle," he said.

"Why?"

"Cuz he's dead," he said, then doubled over laughing.

Those were the days when nothing really mattered because we were about to get drunk and high and laid. Those were the days

127

when we *didn't* get laid, so we ran around town stealing street signs and lawn ornaments. Everything was funny then.

But Eric wasn't laughing now. Death, it seems, is funnier when you're nineteen and on acid than it is when you're fifty and on Lipitor.

WHEN I GRADUATED from Springfield in 1988, Andy gave me a briefcase, which I still have. I used it to carry around writing research for twenty years. I also used it to carry around beer and vodka.

I had it when I met with Henry Kissinger and Governor Pataki for lunch in 1998. It was loaded with beer and vodka.

Lester Millman, the Governor's photographer, was taking pictures of our three-way lunch through the glass walls. A week later, he slid a few photos under my office door. One photo shows me trying to sneak an empty vodka nip into the briefcase right under Pataki and Kissinger's nose.

In 2016, I looked though the briefcase while writing the first book. Before I even opened it, memories started coming back to me.

It flew open one morning while I was walking on 42nd Street in New York City. Three beers fell out and rolled down the busy sidewalk, forcing people to step out of the way. I tried to appear shocked, like I had no idea where all the beer was coming from.

It's amazing. We were on the streets of New York City, where there's a naked homeless guy selling his boogers for booze money, and they're looking at me like a sex offender because I had beer in my briefcase.

I tried using the briefcase to sneak vodka with me to Ground Zero on 9/11. While we were getting out of the Suburban at the World Trade Center, the Governor said, "You should leave that here."

I always wondered why he said that. Maybe he thought it would look suspicious to be walking around in four inches of ashes with a briefcase. Most likely, he knew there was booze in it.

There was absolutely no good place to sneak drinks down there anyway, which means I probably would have gotten caught. Either way, on 9/11 at the World Trade Center, the Suburban was a good place for the briefcase.

I'M NOT ESPECIALLY SENTIMENTAL, but I like to mark certain events. After learning about Andy's death, I printed out his obituary and put it in the briefcase. I'm sure it'll be there forever.

The days of beer and vodka are over. What better place, than in this briefcase that went out of style ten minutes after Andy gave it to me, to put everything – 9/11, alcohol and now Andy -- to rest.

Ironically, stumbling on Andy's death made me realize the value of looking at things from above. I continued to use Google Earth while writing *You Can't Die: A Day of Clarity,* mostly to check facts and study the locations where events took place.

I used it to retrace my getaway route following the altercation with Big Eminem behind the shopping plaza in Guilderland.

For some reason, the speed bump I bashed his head against is gone now. Maybe Big Eminem forced the town to remove it because he needed closure.

Google Earth has no boundaries, of course, so I couldn't resist strolling across the bridge in Tijuana where me and four others were surrounded by Mexican police.

I went to the World Trade Center and hovered over the memorial. From above, Ground Zero looked the same as it did seventeen years ago, a shinier version of hell.

I've never been to the memorial. If I went there, I'd look around trying to remember where things were the day it happened, a pointless exercise that would help exactly zero people.

In 2016, I texted the wife of my friend Brian Sweeny. Brian was there for the few years where drinking actually produced great memories in the early 90s.

He was on one of the hijacked planes that hit the Twin Towers. Just before his plane crashed, Brian left a voice message for his wife, saying he wanted her to move on with her life and be happy.

After writing Brian's story into my first book, she wrote back:

"Count yourself as one of the lucky ones that got to know an amazing man.... even for such a short time. He was a life changer."

Chapter Ten

The Tangled Relationships of AA

TWO YEARS SOBER

Juan was still on probation when we first met, which means he was always one slight screwup from going back to prison. Turning your life around isn't always good enough to satisfy a system that seems eager to keep you on their clipboard.

I wasn't worried that Juan would return to his drunken, gangbanging ways. I was worried that one of the many idiots around him would catch the attention of the police and, one way or the other, the Puerta Rican with the long rap sheet would be the one going to jail.

Here's a safe bet: If Juan's Irish girlfriend with no record hits him in the forehead with a rolling pin, and he defends himself by pushing her away, his bloody, shackled ass is heading to prison.

We were at a meeting together one day when a little chaos broke out. A guy at the back of the room got the impression that a guy named Steven, who was chairing the meeting, disrespected him.

It must have been a well-veiled insult because I didn't hear it – at least, not this time. Steven had a knack for pissing people off with his ill-chosen words.

On his way to kill Steven, the guy shoved chairs and yelled threats and obscenities.

Juan, who was sitting right next to me, went to stand up, presumably to intervene. He was halfway up when I grabbed his shoulder and pulled his ass back down.

He gave me a confused look.

"It's not your problem," I told him. "Not mine either."

This book didn't suddenly become fiction. It's true. This time, I was the pacifist. I was the voice of reason. I was the rational thinker.

Hell, you can even say I was the pussy. My goal for the rest of my life is to be the sober pussy who's not in trouble. I'm not jeopardizing my freedom ever again.

These days, my policy is to run like hell from any situation that could conceivably involve the police. It should have been Juan's policy too, even more so than mine, since he was on probation.

"I was just going to break it up," he said.

"Let someone who's not on probation break it up."

And that's exactly how it turned out. A handful of other members intercepted the guy and dragged him out the door.

"I'm surprised you didn't defend your buddy," Juan said, referring to Steven.

"If someone attacked me, I wouldn't rely on someone else to protect me."

Steven and I used to talk a lot more than we do today. We usually sat together in meetings and texted back and forth on a regular basis – a regular basis by our standards, which means, when there was something to say.

Juan was convinced that Steven sat next to me in meetings, so he could be a wise ass to everyone without getting his ass kicked.

"If that's his theory, it's a bad one," I told Juan. "Someone wanted to kill him today. Not only did I refuse to step in, I stopped you from stepping in too."

Steven is a genetic copy of Eric Jackson. God endowed both with cocksure mouths and too much testosterone. They are either unaware of basic decorum, incapable of it, or they just don't give a shit.

They even walk the same -- with an overconfident strut that most assuredly titillates one percent of the female population while making the other ninety-nine percent want to shoot them in their groins.

Together, their mouths could cause a million divorces and start a civil war between the genders – all fifty-one of them.

After decades of causing all sorts of sexually-driven mayhem, Eric Jackson is slowing down and getting married in Colorado. Steven is still active and spreading his seed in the Glens Falls.

Although Steven comes within striking distance, it's impossible for anyone to be more obnoxious than Eric Jackson was thirty years ago.

In 1987, at a Springfield bar called "The Well," Eric was making his rounds, which entailed asking for sex from as many girls possible, hoping at least one of them would be desperate or drunk enough to say yes.

"It's a numbers game," he used to say.

His MO was well thought out. On campus, he made a point of saying something – anything – to every good-looking female he crossed paths with.

Then, at night, he'd sit on the edge of his bed with a campus phone directory and a highlighter. He'd go in alphabetical order, looking for any girl whose name sounded vaguely familiar, then dial the number and turn on the snake charm.

Obviously, I could only hear his side of the conversation. It always went something like this.

"Hey, it's Eric, from English Lit. How ya doing?"

"Eric Jackson. I sit three rows behind you."

"Yeah, blonde hair... perfect physique."

"Hey, wanna come over to Gulick Hall, just to hang out?"

If the answer was no – and it almost always was – he didn't waste another second of his time on small talk or niceties or politeness or anything aimed at building a rapport in hopes of getting a *yes* the next time.

Instead, he'd find a way to get off the phone as quickly as possible, so he could move on to the next girl.

"Oh crap, I just spilled something on my gigantic penis. I'll talk to you later."

There was no time for long goodbyes when he was bursting under the belt. He had a lot more highlighted numbers to call.

One Saturday night at the Well, Eric ran into one of his "Numbers." She had already said no a few nights earlier, but now that he was drunk, he decided to give it another try.

The Number's boyfriend, who was about three feet away, heard enough of Eric's sex pitch to put him in a fighting mood.

I was at the other end of the bar when I heard a guy's voice yelling at Eric. Well, I assumed the guy was yelling at Eric. I mean, who else would a jealous guy in a bar be yelling at?

It sounded like a threat. The Number was standing right there, and she threw a drink at Eric's chest. He stepped back, laughing it off, like it was all part of his master plan.

A mutual friend of ours, Pete Quinlan, was behind me. He whispered in my ear.

"I hope you realize this is gonna end up being your fight."

Oh yeah, I know that, Juan... I mean, Pete.

SEVENTY-FIVE PERCENT of the ways Eric picked up women in the 1980s would be considered illegal today. One hundred percent of them would get you fired.

Steven gets just as many phone numbers as Eric did – and he does it without violating a dozen laws aimed at protecting women, children, domestic animals and national security.

He also does it without the advantage of a phone directory, but Steven knows a thing or two about working a room.

Alcoholics Anonymous is a bad place to look for sex, but if you want sex and you've got an ounce of charisma, it's an easy place to get it.

In AA, they call that "Thirteenth-Stepping," and a lot of people do it -- but no one does it with the sheer efficiency of Steven.

One night, Steven sent me a text about sex that wound up getting me – not him, but me – in trouble with women. I don't know how that works. He's good.

In the text, he was bragging about his most recent tryst – an attractive blonde woman from the rooms.

"You know her," he kept telling me.

But no matter how much he described her, I couldn't figure out who he was talking about.

The next day, I saw a blonde woman at a meeting. I was pretty sure she was Blondie, the one he was talking about, but I didn't want her to see me whispering in Steven's ear, so I texted him from three feet away.

"Is that the one you were telling me about?"

Steven stood up and pointed right at her.

"Yeah, that's her!"

Now Blondie was looking at us the way a gazelle looks at a lion crouching in the tall grass.

I'm usually quick on my feet, because I'm good at anticipating what people are going to do – but I could never have anticipated this.

I should have just laughed and given Steven credit for a brilliantly-thrown curveball. Instead, I grabbed a shovel and started to dig myself in deeper.

"What are you talking about?"

He held up his phone and literally pointed to my text and stuck it in my face.

"You asked me if that was her. Yeah, that's her."

Motherfucker.

Here's the thing. I didn't care what Blondie thought about all this, but there were several other women in the room, and I didn't want them to think Steven's conquests were a group effort. At this point, I was hoping to cut my losses and end it.

It was going to be tough. I couldn't say, "Oh, okay," because that would be an admission that I cared enough about his sexcapades to ask about her. Worse, it would be an admission that I was lame enough to send him a text right under her nose.

I looked over at Blondie. I shook my head and turned my thumb at Steven as if to say: *What's up with this guy? Do you know what he's talking about? I don't know what he's talking about.*

Then I grabbed my shovel, jumped on it with both feet, and dug a lot deeper.

I leaned into him, pretending to get a closer look at his phone. What I was really doing is getting close enough to whisper, "Okay, you win. Shut the fuck up."

Since I was mad, it didn't come out as a whisper and I think everyone in the room heard it.

Blondie and the other the women weren't cutting me a break. They weren't even trying to hide their interest. They were staring at me, as if I owed them an explanation. They expected this kind of behavior from Steven but, somehow, they got the impression I was more mature than him.

I kept thinking: *How did I become the misogynist in this thing? I was just asking a question. He's the one that was running his mouth.*

I typed another text telling him to "STOP," then shoved the phone three inches in front of his face.

"Stop why?" he yelled, as Blondie watched with daggers in her eyes.

Finally, a group of people came in, Blondie got distracted and the other women stopped staring at me. At that point, I knew why so many people wanted to kill Steven.

Here's the big difference between Eric and Steven. Eric would have done the same thing, just to be a dick. Steven is so devoid of grace and decorum, he didn't even realize he was being a dick.

All of this is said with love, of course. I like these guys, and not just because they provide a steady stream of guilty pleasure and tawdry entertainment. Both are intelligent deep thinkers who understand the human condition as well as anyone. And both are softening with age.

Eric and I talked for a long time on the phone after I told him about Andy's death. He was obviously more emotional than usual. It was the kind of emotion he was incapable of thirty, twenty or even five years ago.

So, when it was time to say goodbye, I showed a little affection.

"Okay, I'll talk to you soon my friend," I told him.

"I love you," he said.

"You gotta be shitting me. What's wrong with you?"

It's probably not the reaction he was shooting for.

I wanted to tell him: Don't change on me just because we're getting old. If you're gonna say something like that, don't say it like you're whispering in your wife's ear or like we're slow dancing.

Say it like this: "Luv ya, douchebag."

I'll get the point and I might even say it back. Or say it in passing, without the little pause first, so it doesn't sound like you've been rehearsing it all day and you're on your knees with a ring, or an open mouth.

I'm writing this, not with a hard and simple mind, but with a smirk. I love Eric Jackson and Charles... and a few other guys, but, see what I mean? When I lay it out there like that, it's smooth and subtle and cool. It's not all... icky.

A FEW WEEKS AFTER the text incident, Steven redeemed himself on my two-year anniversary of being sober. It may not sound like the kind of thing that would mean anything to me, especially since I brushed off my one-year anniversary, but this time was different. Alcoholics Anonymous was starting to grow on me.

Somehow, Steven remembered my sobriety date, and announced it at our home group meeting.

Instead of marking the occasion with a cake, he stuck a big "2" candle in a package of Ho-hos and presented me with a two-year coin and a card. It's precisely the kind of thing I'd do, which is probably why I liked it.

God only knows what the kinder, gentler Eric would have done, but it probably would have included a long, dramatic embrace.

Steven knew better. He handed me my coin, shook my hand and patting me on the back.

Of course, no one is more pragmatic than me. When I chaired his celebration five months later, I found a way to avoid touching him at all. I spoke on his behalf, but had a mutual female friend present him with the coin. He hugged her (too long) as I looked on and gave myself another pat on the back.

Chapter Eleven

The Only Requirement for Membership is what?

MORE THAN TWO YEARS SOBER

Breaking news is no longer news in my world. The big moments keep coming, but it's easier to keep stressful times in perspective these days — especially with my sponsor's oft-repeated refrain ringing my ear. "Does it affect your breathing?"

Mallory was passing through Queensbury one day, and I asked her to meet me, Lisa and Rachel at the gym, so we could go somewhere for dinner. When Mallory got there, she seemed antsier than usual.

Whatever was on her mind, I was going to find out about it right there in the gym.

"Dad I need to talk to you alone for a second."

No parent likes hearing that. It's not the kind of thing your children say before they tell you they won the lotto.

Besides, I don't like being asked to step aside for a private conversation. It guarantees the excluded party is going to pepper me with questions later – especially the two people excluded in this case.

Later, if I tried to tell Lisa it was a private matter, she'd go to bed, no matter what time of day it was. Rachel is worse. She won't go anywhere because she won't take no for an answer. She'll ask and ask and ask until I go to bed, and then she'll ask some more.

Mallory and I went to a quiet area and sat on the massage chairs.

It's amazing how many conclusions you can jump to in the four seconds it takes to walk fifteen feet.

She's joining ISIS. No, not Mallory, she's probably just pregnant. Fuck! She's too young to be a mother, and I'm sure as hell too young to be a grandfather.

Okay, I need to be supportive – yay, I'm going to be a grandfather. Wait a minute. That's it, she's dating a grandfather. I'll kill the dirty old bastard.

Maybe she wants a sex change. Fine, I'll sell the lake house. That makes no sense. None of this makes sense. I hope she's not leaving the country. I'll bet she's moving to North Korea... not with my grandchild she's not! Forget it, Comrade.

We went over to the massage chairs.

"Sit down," she said.

I've gotta be sitting for this? Oh, God, she's going to North Korea. I raised a commie.

"Okay honey, tell me."

"I'm in AA."

"You in a... a... what? In a bind, in a bad mood, in a cult?"

"Dad, I'm in the rooms of AA."

I knew she wasn't joking because of the way she said it – "in the rooms." That's AA jargon, so it was obvious she'd been to some meetings.

At first, I was waiting for the other shoe to drop. When someone her age walks into the rooms of AA, there's always another shoe, and it usually entails getting arrested.

"Honey, what's going on? Do you think you have a problem, or did something happen? I didn't think you drank that much."

The next thing she said came sailing from her mouth *way* too fast, like she was itching to say it.

"Dad, the only requirement for AA membership is a desire to stop drinking."

That's a line from the Alcoholics Anonymous preamble, which is read at the beginning of every meeting. She said it with sort of a snarky, self-satisfied look on her face.

I looked at her phone to see if the red light was blinking. Nope. I wasn't being recorded.

For once, I was having trouble reading her. I didn't know what to say.

As a member of AA, I'm supposed to be happy anytime someone joins the program because millions of people have used it to turn around their lives. But this was my daughter. Her life doesn't need turning around. At least, I didn't *think* it did.

I played it cool.

"You're citing AA literature already? Come on, talk to me."

"I don't like the way I feel the day after I drink, and I think I'd be better off without alcohol in my life, just like you."

It was the perfect answer, whether she was serious or not.

I don't know why I was suspicious of being pranked. It would be a lame joke. Mallory could come up with something better than this.

A few months earlier, Mallory and one of her black friends made a bet. They announced that they were in a serious relationship – even though they weren't -- to see whose family freaked out more.

Hey, I didn't come up with this bet, they did. It seemed outdated by about fifty years to me.

Mallory's performance was smooth. She didn't say he was black; she just told me about him and directed me to a picture of him on Facebook.

"Yeah, we're in a serious relationship and I just wanted you to know."

"No one can accuse me of being racist," I told her. "I only have two friends – one is black, and one is Puerta Rican – and now I'm gonna have a black son-in-law."

In the picture I saw, he was on stage, doing stand-up comedy. At the time, Mallory was doing open mic nights at comedy clubs.

I sent him a friend request on Facebook. We swapped a few funny messages, and that was it.

Apparently, Mallory won the bet because his family took one look at Mallory's picture and lost it. They were so pissed, the friend had to tell them it was a joke in the first thirty seconds.

Honestly, I'm glad it was a joke. I need a lot of attention. What I *don't* need is Chris Rock stealing my laughs.

TO THIS DAY, I don't think Mallory is an alcoholic, but she has the gene and she knows it. Either way, AA is usually the right answer for children of alcoholics, and it's probably the right answer for a lot of non-alcoholics.

The word "alcohol" is only mentioned once in the Twelve Steps. The rest of the program is about living right, being happy and not acting like an asshole.

The last part isn't in the literature, but that's what it amounts to.

My dad dragged me to an AA meeting when I was about Mallory's age. There were about thirty people in the meeting, half men, half women, mostly young.

I spent the entire hour sizing up the women in the room, ranking them from one to ten based on how much I would or would not want to have sex with them.

I doubt that's what Mallory is doing in the rooms of AA. Other than Steven, I can't think of anyone who's doing that in the rooms of AA.

The only thing I was serious about at Mallory's age was keeping Eric Jackson away from my beer and my girlfriends, especially my beer.

It's amazing that me and Mallory hang from the same genetic tree. I guess the males on my side of the family are the low-hanging fruit.

I was forty-six by the time I surrendered to a disease that Mallory confronted before it even presented itself -- at the age of twenty-one.

I'm an entire generation less mature than my daughter, and that's okay with me. There's no greater joy than to be humbled by your children.

I WONDERED IF It would be awkward to go to a meeting with Mallory. A few months later, I decided to find out.

"I'm going to meeting in Hudson Falls. Want to meet somewhere around there?"

"Where's the meeting? I'll be there."

Mallory still hadn't arrived when the meeting started. It was a speaker meeting and the speaker that day was Juan.

I was worried that Mallory would be too shy or afraid to walk in late, especially in this room. It's an intimidating layout for newcomers. When you walk through the door, you're front and center, with thirty or forty people staring at you.

I was about to walk outside to wait for Mallory when the door opened, and she breezed in like she was the landlord coming to collect rent.

That was the day I stopped agonizing about her ordeal two years earlier.

Mallory had persevered. No one had broken her spirit. No one had taken her self-esteem. No one had stolen her soul. She was no one's victim. Not only did she refuse to let it bring her down, she used it to lift herself up, as proof that should could withstand anything.

They say you're only as happy as your unhappiest child. They also say life sucks and then you die. For some unfortunate parents, those sayings are redundant.

Being a parent is a lifetime... no. I was going to say "sentence," but "commitment" is better.

Mallory is proving that being a parent can be a life of rewards instead of a life of work and worry. Jackson is well on his way to proving the same thing. I say, "on his way" because he's still a probationer, aka, a teenager.

He's also the closest thing to me walking around on this planet. With that comes a mixture of curses and blessings. I'll do everything in my power to block the curses, just like my mom did for me and my brother – but a parent can only do so much.

My mother spent way too much of her life agonizing over where my drinking would take me. I feel guilty about that, and she feels guilty that I feel guilty. It's not just alcoholism that runs in the family.

Mom was a fearless guardian from the beginning. She didn't waste time worrying about anything other than the welfare of her children.

In other words, Mallory inherited the gift – and it is a gift – of not giving a shit about what other people think. To be clear, both care about other people; they just don't care about being judged.

When it came to the latter, no one was stronger or more secure than my badass mother.

In 1972, when men still called their waitresses "kitten," my father and two other poorly dressed men were standing in the living room of our house drinking beer and staring out the window.

I was about seven years old and I stood behind them as they watched their wives march across the street to bust up a party.

My dad, clearly moved by my mom's bravery, poked the back of my head and pointed out the window.

"There goes one tough broad."

Mom is a broad?

My mother was leading two other broads into battle against a large crowd of drunken, rowdy teens. They were throwing a loud, unsanctioned beer bash at one of the neighborhood houses.

I didn't want to look out the window because I feared what the wild teens might do to my mom. Instead, I just watched my dad and the other two men as they stared out the window.

I peeked one time, right at the beginning. The two women my mom deputized walked behind her while their spineless husbands and my father drank beer and praised their "spunk."

Then my dad pulled me over to the window and made me watch. I guess he thought it would be educational. Maybe he thought it would inspire me to grow up and be a man... like my mom.

I'll never forget how scared I was when my mom walked up the front steps with her *ipso edita* no-knock warrant and barged through the front door.

"This should be interesting," said one of the pussies beside me.

Almost instantly, the loud music stopped. Suddenly, teens came pouring out of the house. Some were running.

My mom didn't come out right away and I was crying because I thought they killed her. Turns out, they were more afraid of her than she was of them. She didn't come out immediately. Most likely, she was making sure they all left. I can see her going room to room, kicking down doors.

Eventually, the three bellbottom-wearing 70s chicks sashayed right back to our house to thank the brave men in their lives.

I wonder if, while my mom was in the house, there was a wall with writing on it, and I wonder if she saw the writing on that wall. I wonder if she had a premonition that this was just the preamble to lifetime of dealing with alcoholics and their shitty behavior.

As a boy, a year or two later, I remember a drunk patient taking a swing at her when she was an emergency room nursing supervisor.

"Don't worry," she told me. "That's what people do when they drink too much."

Then she was promoted to Director of a unit called Entry to Care, which dispatched vans across the streets of Rochester to pick up homeless drunks, then brought them back to a sobering-up facility where they had to face my mother.

That'll ruin a perfectly good beer buzz. Trust me.

Mom, apparently a glutton for punishment, went on to become a Director at Parkridge Hospital Chemical Dependency, then finished her career leading Monroe County's Department of Mental Health.

Back in 1972, my 29-year-old mom busted up that drunken bash because she knew it was scaring me. Exactly forty years later, in 2013, she sat at the foot of my bed in the intensive care unit, watching her son nearly die from alcoholism.

She stayed by my bed the whole time I was there, quizzing and consulting every nurse, doctor and orderly that came within ten feet of me.

My mom has spent every day of her adult life fighting alcoholism -- not her own, everyone else's. It's a miracle she didn't turn to booze herself.

In fact, now that everyone around her is sober and happy, isn't it her turn to let loose? Shouldn't she be on a victory cruise around the world, gambling, smoking ganja and taking drunk selfies?

You'd think the last place she'd want to be is working as a volunteer in a Florida hospital. But, who else is going to volunteer their time to comfort addicted newborns? Who better to hold babies suffering through excruciating withdrawal from heroin, meth and whatever else their mothers were addicted to?

It's a shitty way to come into this world, but my mom is there for them, just as she was there for me.

What's the reward for a lifetime dedicated to fighting other peoples' addictions?

In 2015, almost two years after I left rehab, my family got together at my mom's summer place on Canandaigua Lake.

My mom was basking in her glory. She had her entire family – children, grandchildren, everyone -- together for a day of boating on the lake. We took turns tubing and laughing at whoever's turn it was to get victimized by my brother, who was steering the boat into figure eights and sending everyone flying dangerously through the air. The whole family was sober and happy.

For my mom, it was pure bliss. It's the moment she'd been dreaming of for decades.

No one deserved this day more than her, but no one has lousier luck either. The way the rest of the day went down is proof that life's not always fair. If it was, John Lennon would still be making music, and Madonna wouldn't.

As my mom was stepping into the boat, she lost her footing and fell straight down between the dock and boat, right onto the steel infrastructure of the hoist.

On the way down, her head slammed against the metal cross frame. It was as bad as it sounds.

There were about six of us there, looking down at her, horrified and hysterical, trying to figure how bad she was hurt, where the blood was coming from and how we were going to raise her up and out of the water.

She was standing chest-deep in the water holding on to the same metal beam that caught her head on the way down.

She was conscious but not saying anything. The pain must have been excruciating, but she never made a sound or changed the expression on her face. She just stood there under the dock and boat with a thousand-yard stare.

I know my mom. She was doing two things.

The nurse in her was evaluating everything she could feel, especially her head injury, to determine how badly she was hurt. At the same time, she was holding it all in, the pain as well as the fear – not the fear of being seriously hurt, but the fear of her dream day coming to an early end.

Again, I know her. As soon we extricated her from this soaking mousetrap, she would downplay the whole thing and say it was time for lunch.

Me and my brother finally lifted her up through the narrow space between the dock and boat. Lisa ran a few hundred yards back to my mother's summer camp for first aid stuff.

There was a lot of blood. Some bystanders and neighbors came over to help. We were taking turns examining her on a picnic table. The consensus was that we needed to get her to the hospital for stitches and a possible concussion.

That's when my 82 Airborne brother, trying to lighten the hysteria, chimed in with his treatment recommendation.

"Just rub some dirt in it."

I know what he was trying to achieve, but he didn't achieve it. That psychology may have worked in Panama and Iraq, but in Canandaigua, it went over like a loud vibrator in church.

My mother twisted her bloody head around and gave him a look that would have ruined the rest of his life if he had seen it. Then she glanced at me to make sure I wasn't laughing.

I'm not that stupid. As soon as I felt her head turning my way, I looked down and shook my head in disgust at my brother's obscene insensitivity.

It really wasn't that funny. It would have been funnier if he was pretending to inspect the boat, making sure mom didn't damage it with her head.

My mom was checked out at the hospital then released, and then she did what I predicted – acted like nothing happened.

She's got a hard head, in more ways than one.

When hurricane Irma was bearing down on her house in Spring Hill, Florida, I was glued to the weather channel. At first, they said Irma was going to pound the east coast of Florida.

Then, about a day before Irma touched down near Miami, Irma changed course and headed towards the west coast. Spring Hill was right in its path.

The last time I talked to my Mom before the storm hit, she seemed surprised that I was calling twice in one day.

"Oh, hello... again."

"Hello again? You realize this hurricane is heading straight towards you, right? Is your will in a safe place?"

"I'm so tired of all this storm coverage. I can't get anything else on TV."

"Mom! You're about to get blown away! I know it's too late to evacuate, but what are you and Laurie *[Larimore, my stepfather]* doing to prepare?"

"Well, he's trying to block the front door with a table," she said, mockingly.

Every news outlet in America was predicting that Irma would leave a trail of devastation in its path up the west coast of Florida. They said Tampa and Spring Hill would sustain a "direct hit."

I was scared – probably as scared as I was forty years earlier when she marched across the street to bust up the beer bash.

"Mom, are you taping the windows?"

Mom couldn't be bothered. She sounded like a teenager being snotty to her parents.

"I'm not doing *anything*."

In 1989, she and my dad came to a Who concert with me. A fight broke out near us and I tried to step in front of her to block her from the fray.

My Mom yanked her arm back and looked at me like I insulted her.

"You think I'm afraid of *them*?"

Everyone else was getting out of the way, but mom wasn't moving for anyone.

"Mom, just step over here for a minute until it's over."

She shook her head at me, like she was disappointed in herself for raising such a pussy.

I'm surrounded by steel magnolias.

Lisa's steeliness and strength presents itself in a different way, in the form of loyalty — loyalty that is often devoted to people who've done nothing to earn it, like me five years ago.

Lisa was bluffing with a shitty hand when she gambled on me, and the jury is still out on the size of the pot.

I made out damn well; there's no question about that.

When I first showed her competition pictures to my friends in AA, they all reacted the same way. They'd stare at her picture for a while, then stare at me, searching for whatever it is she could possibly see in me.

I always point to my private area and say, "It matters."

Lisa fights for those who fight for themselves. She doesn't care how far down the scale they've fallen. She will not give up on them. If the person still wants to win, Lisa will root them on into perpetuity, even if they continue to lose. If they are still trying, Lisa will stay in their corner. My wife never throws in the towel.

Another thing the jury is still deliberating is whether her son, my stepson, inherited all those characteristics. He inherited the

155

loyalty part, but it's hard to use the same fighting metaphors on him.

I could only come up with one: Michael is constantly punching above his weight class. He's got the bellowing voice for it, but the other part is still a work in progress. The problem is that he thinks the angry voice is enough.

I've told him a million times… if you're going to bluff a guy into thinking you're tough, don't do it by running up and roaring him. Yeah, he might get scared and run away, but if he wants to fight, you're screwed.

After an incident in a bowling alley one night, I reminded him to do as I say, not as I do.

Chapter Twelve

The Wrath of Grapes

TWO AND A HALF YEARS SOBER

"Did you see that?" screamed Michael.

"Yeah," I said. "Who was that guy?"

"I have no idea... just some drunk douchebag."

After two years of hearing the Serenity Prayer in meetings, it was time for the ultimate test: using it.

This guy didn't just touch my stepson's ass; he owned it. His hand started at the bottom of Michael's butt, then went down, under and up... right to Michael's dangly grapes.

We were in a bowling alley when it happened. At first, I thought the guy was an older cousin or a "funny uncle," and I laughed because... well, because it was funny.

Michael's body lurched straight up, like he stepped on a live wire, and he let out a high-pitched peep, like a duckling's first chirp after pecking its way out of the egg.

I wasn't sure what to do.

One of the Twelve Promises of AA is, *"We will intuitively know how to handle situations which used to baffle us."* I'm sure this isn't the kind of situation the founders of AA had in mind. When the Twelve Promises were written in the 1930s, grabbing another man's ass would get you killed or carted away to the nearest sanitarium.

These days, what happened to Michael is considered a sexual assault. If it happened to me, I'd never report the "attacker" to the police. I'd either beat him senseless or get his phone number. It depends on the guy.

Michael would have to settle for getting a phone number. Even at six-foot-two, he wasn't ready to pound the crap out of anyone. I mean, when the guy's hand went into Michael's butt, he squealed like a violated penguin. It wasn't the sound of a fighter.

So, now I was the one who had to do something.

It's not the kind of thing I wanted to fight over. It's too weird. Besides, it was too late. You can't respond to something like this with words. What could I say... *Hey, you molested him?* It was too late to tackle him and claim I was defending Michael.

But, as his stepfather, I couldn't just let it go entirely.

By the time I figured out what was going on, Happy Hands and his drunken crew were almost to the front door, which meant I had to run to catch up to them, attracting the kind of attention I've been trying to avoid since I got out of rehab three years earlier.

"Stay here," Jackson told Michael. "I'll stop him from killing someone."

The group of three guys and one woman were near the front desk when I got to them. I ran up behind them and jabbed Happy Hands in the back.

"You! What were you thinking?"

As always, I could hear Jackson in the background.

"Dad! Don't do it!"

I *wasn't* going to do it. That's the old me. The new me was trying to look mad without laughing my ass off. The new me wasn't even thinking of the guy I just jabbed in the back. The new me was thinking of ways to make fun of Michael when we got in the car.

I mean, Michael's a tall seventeen-year-old man, kind of. Why isn't he bashing this guy's head in with a bowling pin? Why is he letting his 50-year old stepfather defend his honor?

The guy was still trying to decide what he was going to do about me jabbing him in the back. I got nice and close to him, so he'd have to step back to take a swing.

"You just grabbed my son's ass!"

That might have been the hardest thing I've ever had to say.

I promoted Michael to the blood-rank of "son" to make it more personal. It would also help justify any violence that might take place.

The alley manager was nervous. He kept yelling at the group.

"Just go, hurry up and get out!"

I was pretty sure the guy would back down, and he did. He pretended to not know what I was talking about, which is fine. I still made him apologize for it, and he did that too.

Problem is, I told him to apologize to *Michael*, but he didn't know what Michael looked like because he'd only seen, and felt, Michael's ass. So, he wandered around the front desk apologizing to everyone else in the bowling alley. Michael was nowhere in sight. After Happy Hands and his crew left, Jackson and I found him. He was about as far away from the confrontation as he could get.

The incident wasn't really a test of my sober serenity. I wasn't even mad, so achieving serenity was easy. The hardest part was trying not to laugh.

A real test of my sober serenity would have been him doing the same thing to Mallory. He wouldn't have been able to apologize for that. I'd have hit him till he stopped moving.

If it had been Jackson, I'd have told the guy, "You have a choice between who's going to pound your head in – me or my son. But if you pick him and he starts to lose, I'll join in."

That's not gender bias. I don't care what anyone says. There's a difference between boys and girls, sons and daughters and men and women.

If that had happened to Mallory or Rachel or Lisa, I wouldn't have called them sluts or told them they were asking for it by wearing tight jeans. But that's what I told Michael.

In fact, we were less than five feet out the door when the ball busting began. He was surprised I waited that long.

"So, Michael, let me ask you something..."

"Here we go," he said.

"Why were you hiding behind the Ms. Pac Man machine? Did you lose a quarter?"

Jackson defended Michael by mocking me.

"It's always the same with my dad," he said, while doing a grossly exaggerated imitation of me when I confront people.

He put his arms back (which I would never do) and puffed out his chest (which I never do) and stomped around like a bully (which I'm not), carrying on like Gunnery Sergeant Hartman in Full Metal Jacket (I love that guy).

I will give you exactly three fucking seconds to wipe that stupid grin off your face, or I will gouge out your eyeballs and skull-fuck you!

Mr. Kubrick, you and I could have done great work together.

THE WHOLE RIDE HOME, I referred to Michael as "Michele," and compared him to my first girlfriend.

I'm not proud of any of this, by the way. I'm just reporting what happened, and what I was like two and a half years into recovery. It's generally accepted that chronic alcoholism stunt's a person's emotional maturity, and I've spent the past four years proving it.

It's all in fun, but it's teenage fun, not middle-age golfing and hunting fun. I don't want to golf and hunt. I'd rather snort playdough. I've tried golf and I hated it. I've never tried hunting and I never will. There's a few people I would mind shooting, but I wouldn't shoot anything else unless it was attacking me.

I've read about severe cases, where people stop maturing the moment they start using alcohol. I guess that makes sense. If you drink to deal with social situations instead of learning how to deal with them the right way, you're not maturing.

So, when an alcoholic – especially an extreme case, like me -- finally quits drinking, their maturity can – *can* -- regress to the time when they began drinking. It happens.

Here's how the math on that shakes out for me: I'm eighteen again.

The good news is that when I'm with Jackson and Michael, I don't have to adjust my behavior to fit in. The bad news is obvious. Lisa can't take me anywhere.

Fortunately, there's one place where erratic behavior is the norm, and stunted maturity is the cover charge for getting in the door.

THE COLORFUL WORLD of AA is a good place to harvest material for a book. That's assuming you know how to do it without blowing the lid of a program whose inviolate principle is anonymity. Since I can, here's another glimpse of the funniest nut show ever produced.

My friend George, who has been in the program for about a year, is constantly talking about producing a sitcom. I'm not sure George is producer material. He's more of a pilot program whose Nielsen ratings are still being tabulated. Besides, AA is more of a series of still shots, like courtroom sketches, rather than moving pictures.

I wish I could paint because there are certain snapshots in time that belong on canvas. One of them materialized one Saturday night at a big speaker meeting in a giant Glens Falls church.

There were about thirty-five of us that night and there were two speakers. The first speaker was about ten minutes into his very emotional story when a woman's voice rang out.

"Aaaaahhh! Is that a bird?"

It wasn't a bird, unless it was one of those rare birds with whiskers, teeth and sonar.

The bat must have flown down the main staircase. Once he came through the big doors and into the large meeting room, there weren't a lot of places for him to fly back out.

Now it was circling the room, occasionally swooping down and forcing people to duck.

It took people longer than it should have to figure out it wasn't a bird. Once they did, they either covered their heads, shrieked or bolted for the stairs, which made no sense because that's where the bat came from.

It's weird. When everyone thought it was a bird, they were laughing. As soon as they heard the word "bat," it was as if someone tossed a grenade in the room.

There's something about a bat that makes people lose their minds. Whenever people see one, they act like LSD freaks running away from raindrops.

It was the funniest thing I'd seen since an emu got loose and forced Jackson's elementary school into lockdown. (Between emus and me, there were a lot of lockdowns at that school.)

Three girls who were close to the door pulled their shirts over their heads (yeah) and made a run for it. They didn't just run; they vanished, never to be seen or heard from again.

But, it's a myth that all girls are afraid of bats.

Madeline is a scrappy, Woodstock-aged woman who's always digging into her purse for something, and I'm always afraid it's a gun.

I was surprised to see her running out the door with the other chickenshits. I expected her to snatch the thing out of the air and give it the Ozzy Osbourne treatment.

Turns out, she wasn't running; she was looking for a weapon, and thirty seconds later, she came back with the only one she could find -- a mop.

Someone's Higher Power must have been hitting the pipe that night. If I didn't know any better, I'd have thought Madeline was back in the 60s, tripping on acid as she swung the mop in the air, even when the bat was on the other side of the room.

The mop head must have been damp, because it was clearly too heavy for her to control. Each time she swung the thing, her body went with it. The bat was in no danger.

If she had swung that mop for another million years, she'd never hit anything but walls and alcoholics.

But, thanks to Mit, there was *nothing to fear but fear itself.* He was manning the doors like a Palace Guard, ready to jump into action if something else wandered through the door, like a Komodo Dragon or a Pterodactyl.

Mit, a rotund old-timer with a scruffy face and interesting hair, keeps half of his belongings on the lanyard around his neck -- everything from keys to a flashlight and a toaster.

He had both of his pudgy hands on the big oak doors, ready to slam them shut when the bat flew back up the stairs. It was a risky job, but someone had to step up and stare defiantly into the jaws of death.

What started as a crowd of thirty-five men and women was now a crowd of twenty cowering alcoholics in danger of relapsing. Most of them were still in their seats, crouched over looked like passengers in a plane that's about to crash.

One asshole took off his shirt, balled it up and tried throwing it in the bat's path to net it. I was that asshole. I'm not sure why I bothered to do anything. I like bats, and I wouldn't have killed it. I probably would have kissed it, just to freak everyone out.

It was fitting that we were in a church because only God could have created such a masterpiece. It was reminiscent of Da Vinci's "Last Supper," or Coolidge's "Dogs Playing Poker."

Had Norman Rockwell been in the room, every man cave in America today would have an "Alcoholics Playing Bat-gammon" rug hanging on the wall.

It's a scene that represents everything that makes AA interesting. It also represents the pool of characters that now comprises my social network. They make life interesting, and that's what my life needs — a lot of interesting, harmless chaos.

Almost all my friends are in AA or NA. In other words, my social circle is almost entirely made up of addicts and alcoholics. To some, that may sound depressing. It only sounds that way.

It's the life I left behind that was depressing. If you're a hardcore alcoholic, there's nothing fun about drinking. It's just something you've gotta do to get through every little moment of the day.

It would be truly depressing if my social circle was like it was five years ago. It was limited to the last person I truly identified with when I was drinking. He hung himself. People in recovery aren't depressing. I'd rather hang with them than him.

Chapter Thirteen

George's Curiosity
THREE YEARS SOBER

In the thirty years since I graduated from Springfield College, I've only met two other Springfield grads, and I met them both in AA -- a fun fact you won't see in Springfield's recruiting literature.

They must be putting something in the campus water tower, like vodka. Or maybe Springfield College students get drunk to forget they're in the scuzziest city in America. It's like Tijuana with an annoying New England accent.

One of Springfield College's most prominent alcoholics is George, a popular, well-known figure in and around Hudson Falls. He graduated from Springfield College five years before me, then did what most Springfield grads do: he coached wrestling and football.

After thirty years of coaching, he did what a lot of other Springfield grads do: Step One: *He admitted he was powerless over alcohol, that his life had become unmanageable.*

After he took a drunken tumble down the stairs of his home, his family coaxed him into Conifer Park, a rehab I'd been to thirteen years earlier. It appears to have had more of an impact on George than it had on me.

I met George the day he walked into his first AA meeting. It was in Hudson Falls, where he was universally known and well respected.

It was a bold way, and a bold place, for George to admit he was an alcoholic. He knew that everyone would either know him or know who he was the second he walked through the door. And yet, after a few meetings, George wasn't even sure if he was an alcoholic. A lot of times, the alcoholic is the last one to know, or the last one to admit it.

About a week after he first walked into the program, George and I were in my car heading to a meeting in Saratoga – the first meeting we'd gone to together – when he popped the big question.

"How do you know when you're an alcoholic?"

"How do *I* know or how do *you* know?"

As a rule, if you're wondering whether you're an alcoholic, you probably are. Most people don't wander into AA because drinking is improving their lives. That's what I told George. But he insisted I ask him some evaluation-type questions.

"When you start drinking, can you stop?" I asked him.

"No."

"What time do you start drinking?"

"In the morning, but just enough to take away the shakes."

"You're an alcoholic."

"You think so?"

"You just got out of a rehab that you checked yourself into voluntarily," I reminded him. "If you didn't think you were an alcoholic, why did you go... to meet new people?"

George reminds me of Andy. I'm not saying he's gay like Andy, and I'm not saying he's not. I'm just saying he reminds me of Andy. He's friendly, outgoing and charismatic. He walks into the local coffee shop and starts shaking hands and asking names.

What he's really doing is entering information into the database that is his big fat Greek head. Shake his hand once and he'll remember it forever. Tell him about your family, and he'll remember that too.

When it's time to recall the information, he freezes and looks up. He'll be walking in a parking lot and suddenly he'll need to retrieve something from his database. He'll stop dead in his tracks, stand straight up, put his fingers up to his head and stay frozen until the thought is complete. The first time he did it in front of me, I thought he was having a stroke. It's a good thing he wasn't because I'm not sure what I'd do about resuscitating him.

It's no coincidence that George doesn't watch TV or the news. He doesn't know that they're enforcing the rules against unwanted touching these days.

George doesn't touch me as *much* as Andy did. The problem is that he touches me the *way* Andy did... so once is too many times. I'm constantly having to swat his big hairy Greek paws off my back and butt. Aisling has the same problem with George, although I'm not sure she thinks it's a problem. More on her later.

THEN THERE'S BRIAN, another football and wrestling coach who graduated from Springfield College. I'm not sure what our alma mater did to stack the rooms of AA with its alumni, but they should probably start having meetings right on campus.

Around the time the three of us met, we began getting together at Dunkin Donuts for an hour before meetings.

Old timers saw us walking into the rooms together, and they loved the fact that three Springfield grads, all wrestlers, found each other in AA. They thought our trio represented the strength and unity of the program. And it did.

But then George had to get all syrupy about it.

He showed up to Dunkin Donuts one day with a friendship puzzle he created the night before. It was based on Springfield College's seal, which is a triangle whose sides are constructed with the words "spirit," "mind," and "body."

Around campus, geeky jocks who embodied the "Spirit, Mind and Body" ideal – whatever that is -- were derided as "triangles."

In hindsight, those "triangles" were smart athletes. I'm not sure what we were mocking them for. Oh wait... now I remember. John Cena, the WWE wrestler, was a Springfield grad, and he was the quintessential triangle. He's also a self-righteous blowhard. That's what we were mocking.

George must have forgotten about the pejorative nature of the triangle. One night he cut a piece of cardboard into three legs of a triangle and labeled them, "Spirit," "Mind," and "Body."

He showed up to Dunkin Donuts the next day with his project and an unusually giddy look on his face.

Brian and I were dumbfounded when he pulled out the three strips of cardboard and laid them on the table. We looked at each other. *What the fuck is he doing?*

He laid each of them upside down -- one in front of Brian, one in front of me, and one in front of himself.

"Okay," he said. "Now turn them over."

I turned over my piece of cardboard. It said, "Mind."

Brian was staring at his, confused. He looked at me and I flashed him my piece of cardboard. He looked back down at his, then flashed his at me.

It said "Spirit."

There was a long pause, and then it got longer.

"Okay," George said. "So, Brian is spirit, John is mind, and I'm body. Now put them on the table."

We put our pieces down and George swept them into the center of the table and arranged them into the shape of a triangle.

"Now, the three of us will keep our side of the triangle as a sign of our friendship."

Crickets.

I don't know why I'm telling this story. By the time it's over, George is going to be the sympathetic character and Brian and I are going to come off as heartless, testosterone-sniffing pigs.

Keep in mind, holding back laughter is harder for some people than it is for others. For me, it's almost impossible, partly because I don't try hard enough. It happens to me at wakes and funerals all the time. The more taboo the place, the harder it is to not laugh.

I don't want to laugh; I just can't control it, like drinking.

Me and Brian continued to stare at the triangle, as George waited patiently, looking at us, then looking down at the triangle, then looking up at us again, and so on.

He was like an eager puppy.

Even if the three of us had been in a war together, something this maudlin would be grossly unacceptable male behavior. In George's defense, he hadn't known me and Brian long enough to know we were assholes. He was about to find out.

Me and Brian looked at George. He was waiting for a response. His face was earnest and sincere. He was so excited, so proud of himself.

I wanted to run to the bathroom and hide. I didn't want to laugh. Scratch that. I didn't want to be the *first one* to laugh. I looked at Brian, but I couldn't make eye contact with him because he was massaging his forehead and looking down at his phone, which wasn't even on.

George was smiling. He kept looking at the triangle then looking at me and Brian, waiting for us to whip out our pom poms and sing the school song.

I wanted to say something to make Brian laugh first, but it had to be something only he would know was sarcastic.

This is the coolest thing ever! Now we can consecrate our friendship every day with this awesome cool cardboard triangle.

But there was no way I was going to get that out of my mouth without laughing, so I didn't try.

I looked out the window at the empty General Electric building across the street where hundreds of people were laid off. I remember feeling awful about the local families that were displaced when that happened. It was sad, and I tried concentrating on the layoff and how unfunny it was. And because I truly felt bad for those families, my strategy for not laughing was working.

But then I looked at Brian again. Now he was looking up at George, squinting his eyes. It looked like he was going to say something.

A smirk was slowly starting to form on his face. I prayed he would burst out laughing so I would look like the good guy. His lips opened slightly two or three times like he wanted to say something, but then he changed his mind.

Then George spoke again.

"What do you guys think?"

Brian looked like his hernia was on fire. His forehead was fire engine red. Finally, Brian broke the silence.

"Geez coach... I don't know what to..."

And with that, Brian lost it. Tears, sweating, trouble breathing... the whole nine yards. He kept trying say more, but it came out like an incomplete sentence of dolphin sounds because he couldn't stop laughing long enough to catch his breath. I thought I was going to have to do CPR on him.

I was doing the same thing, of course, but it's hard to describe what I was doing because I was doubled over with my eyes closed and fluids coming out of at least four holes of my body (I'm counting my eyes as two holes).

George's expression never changed. He was still smiling like a kindergartner showing his parents a neato school project. He had no idea what was happening in the minds of the insensitive pricks across the table.

Brian and I started to feel guilty right around the same time. I tried to make it right.

"No, no, George, seriously," I said, "This was a good idea."

But Brian ruined it.

"We should exchange rings, too."

Then the walls came crashing down. This time I was gasping for air and lost my balance, almost falling off my chair. My hand hit the floor, and I pushed myself up and ran to the bathroom.

I was in there way too long.

I came out once and peeked around the corner to see if Brian had composed himself yet. When he finally did, I went out... but after a few seconds, the whole thing erupted again. That's how we spent the rest of the hour.

As soon as the whole thing started, George's demeanor went from an excited puppy to a puppy in a small cage with no bone.

I tried to fix it. At least ten times afterwards, I said, "No seriously George, this is really cool."

He wasn't having it.

"You guys are assholes."

Here's the part where I try to justify my own narrowminded insensitivity by claiming that 3.5 billion other men are just as bad, which isn't true... but about half of them are.

Most guys won't pass up a golden opportunity to bust another guy's balls. Unlike a lot of women, we don't do it behind their backs. We do it right then and there. It's more fun that way.

All long, I thought George's gesture was nice, and I was glad he valued our friendship – but I wasn't going to tell him that.

Someday, I'd tell him my own way, without all the cardboard and dramatics. I'd end a conversation with something like, "Good talking to you, my friend. Glad to have you in my life. I'll see your ugly ass tomorrow."

Something like that.

Chapter Fourteen

When Life Gives You Lemons
THREE YEARS AND THREE MONTHS SOBER

Much of this book has to do with immaturity. A lot of people call me crazy, but they do it jokingly, unaware that my doctor calls me the same thing. He just uses a different term.

But, as Forest Gump might say, "Crazy is as crazy does." Have you watched television lately? Pay attention to the commercials that sway people, and the reality shows that entertain them. I may be crazy, but I've got an earth full of company.

Still, after a lifetime of drinking, some things are gone forever. Days, weeks, months and even a few years have been redacted from my life like an FBI memo. Then there are other things -- sophistication, couth and sound judgment -- that I never developed while I was drinking.

Apparently, alcohol impedes the growth of these dispositions. I'm not psychoanalyzing myself. Other people have done it for me, and I'm just repeating their conclusions. Is it valid? My wife would know better than me.

When I suddenly hand Lisa my phone while I'm driving, she knows three things are about to happen.

1) I'm getting ready to pull over;

2) I'm going to do something unacceptable or even illegal in public;

3) I'm going to make her record it.

One day we were driving around with a toilet in the back of the car. The way I see it, there are a million ways to entertain my friends and family with a toilet. Don't I owe to them?

We were bringing the toilet up to the lake house, but first we stopped at the gym, which is in the mall.

As we were leaving, I handed Lisa my phone, stopped the car, lifted the toilet out of the back and set it up in the middle of the parking lot where everyone in every direction could see it.

I grabbed a copy of my book from the car, pulled down my pants, and sat down on the toilet. It was right in front of Sears, Dicks and Target. People were starting to stare.

Lisa was unfazed. She wasn't laughing or rushing to get it done. For her, it was business as usual.

"Should I zoom in or do you want the Dicks sign in the background?"

"Let's try it both ways, honey."

Lisa did her thing, snapping pictures from several different angles. Her husband was sitting on a toilet in the middle of a crowded mall parking lot and people were watching. She didn't even giggle. It was becoming increasingly hard to get a reaction out of my wife.

"I got a bunch of shots," she said. "The wide shots look better."

"Thanks, you can go back to the car while I clean up."

"Don't forget to pull up your pants."

We were done and on our way in less than five minutes.

"Okay," she said. "I need coffee."

I loaded the toilet in the back and we headed to the nearest Dunkin' Donuts drive-thru. I ordered the usual.

"Yes, I'd like an extra-large coffee with just cream and a toasted almond black."

"That'll be $5.97. You can go ahead and pull up."

Apparently, it was going to be one of those days. I recognized the girl's voice. I offended her one day when I was trying to be funny. Now, I was hoping she wouldn't remember me when I pulled up.

A few weeks earlier, I went to pay her for a coffee and she was all cheerful and chirpy.

"I don't need your money because the person in front of you paid for you."

"Really?" I said.

"It's part of a wonderful trend today," she said.

"That's awesome," I said. "Then I'll pay for the next person in line."

While she was getting drinks and ringing things up, I looked in the rear-view mirror at the people behind me. It was a big scuzzy-looking dude with a cigarette dangling from his mouth. He was yelling at the woman next to him, sticking his finger in his face. I watched closely to see if he'd cross the line and give me an excuse to intervene. Then the Dunkin Donuts girl came back.

"He's got lots of donuts and drinks, so it'll be $13.34."

"Tell the pig behind me he ruined the wonderful trend," I said.

I was trying to be funny, but she didn't laugh when it happened three weeks ago, and now I was a little embarrassed to face her again, which is fascinating since I wasn't embarrassed at all to sit on a toilet with my pants down in a parking lot just a few minutes earlier.

I don't need Lisa to keep me sober; I just need her. People see our antics on Facebook and say things like, "I want to come live with you guys."

First of all, no you don't. Is the laughter at our house constant? Yeah, pretty much. But where there's laughter, there's usually a victim, and it's never me.

Lisa is constantly putting pictures of me on Facebook. Not too long ago, one of her friends sent her a message.

"Is he always like that?"

It's kind of a loaded question that could be interpreted a million ways. Lisa answered it brilliantly.

"Yes."

Another good response would have been, "Has he always been like what?"

IN THE WINTER OF 2016, the Glens Falls area got pounded so hard with snow, I could barely get the snow blower out of the garage. Instead of being a man and shoveling a little path to get it started, I went inside and had coffee.

Lisa, Michael and Rachel were all home because everything was closed. All three of them were lounging around with their "devices." Their faces were so close to the phones, it looked like they were doing lines off the screens.

Law and Order wasn't on. I checked my three favorite stations, only to find my least favorite shows:

Criminal Minds – five federal bureaucrats in a perpetual intellectual dick-measuring contest.

Law and Order SVU (with Olivia as a lieutenant) – That show jumped the shark five seasons ago. I'm surprised Ice T didn't jump too... off a bridge.

CSI Miami – It's like they're filming everything through an orange filter, so everything matches David Caruso's hair.

Marriage Boot Camp – proof that Americans are getting dumber.

I was so bored, I Googled Betty White, just to make sure she was still alive.

Bam had a bone. I had nothing. The snow was coming down hard. There was two feet of it on the driveway, a foot of it on the road and not a plow truck in sight.

Two things were certain: One, I wasn't going anywhere, at least not in my four-cylinder, two-wheel drive Kia Soul. Two, at some point, the plows would come by and leave a Trump-size wall of snow at the end of the driveway.

Then I wondered what the plow guys would do if I was running a lemonade stand out there.

First things first.

"Honey, do we have lemons?"

"Lemons for what?" Lisa yelled back.

"Can I tell you later?"

"I'm sure I'll find out on my own. I think we have lime juice."

I decided lime juice was fine. I'd just have to add a lot of sugar.

To this day, I'm proud of my big yellow sign -- "Lemonade 25 cents" -- and my handmade money container with the big green dollar sign on the front.

I trudged through the snow and set up shop at the end of the driveway, probably too close to the road. I made a hole in the snow, just big enough to accommodate me, my chair and my lemonade table. Consistent with the summer theme, I was wearing a tank top and shorts.

They plowed the street once already, about five hours earlier, but it was snowing hard and I knew they would be back.

I sat there, waiting. After fifteen minutes, not one car came by, which wasn't surprising given the foot of snow on the road. I didn't sell any lemonade that day, which is good since I didn't have any.

A plow finally came by. There were two guys in it. They stopped fifty feet before they reached the lemonade stand to avoid blowing me off my chair with the tsunami of heavy snow flying off the blade.

The whole point of the lemonade stand was to satisfy my own curiosity about what the plow guys would do. I was bored enough to find out, which means I was out there for my entertainment, not theirs.

I got my answer. They leaned out the window, waved their hands and laughed their asses off. That's what I thought they'd do.

My freelancing wife fired off a photo of my lemonade stand to Albany's NBC affiliate. She does that a lot. I'll be dirty dancing in front of my computer – grinding, twerking and gettin' jiggy with it – and by the time I'm done, it's on Facebook.

That's fine, but, like I said, I just wanted to see what the plow guys would do. Reactions... I live for reactions.

The TV station was all over the snowy lemonade stand, and the next day, wherever I went, I was badgered with the same thing.

"Hey John, can I get some lemonade – *ha ha ha*."

I'm currently taking applications for more clever friends.

Anyway, that's the new and improved mood spike. No fighting, no attacking lawyers, no overdoses... just lemons and snow.

Like the toilet in the parking lot, it barely raises an eyebrow in our house. Rachel said Lisa saw me plodding through the snow with lemonade and tables.

"Oh yeah? What'd your mother say?" I asked.

"Nothing, why?"

Can you imagine how discouraging that is for someone who moves mountains just to see his people's reactions? I'm dragging a lemonade sign and a fucking banquet table through the snow and my wife says nothing? What a bitch... life is.

IN AA, WE TALK about "going to any lengths to stay sober." For me, that means going to any lengths to stay interested, amused and entertained. Boredom isn't a good thing for me. It's not enough to make me drink, but it's a leading contributor of relapses. That's why I'm constantly fighting against it.

I swear a lot. I'm vile. I like grossing people out. I intentionally say things to make people feel uncomfortable – and I do it while recording their reactions.

And when people come to me with trivial problems, instead of indulging them, I remind them that they are going to die anyway so it doesn't really matter. These are just some of the horrible things I do to entertain myself.

Sometimes when I'm talking freestyle – freestyle means I'm saying whatever I want, which is usually -- my Mother-In-Law looks at me with squinty eyes, like she's trying to figure out what species I am.

Or she'll lean into me, like my words are close-captioned in tiny letters on my forehead, and she's having trouble reading it. There's nothing wrong with her sight. She's just wondering what the fuck I'm talking about. Most times, I'm not talking about anything; I'm just looking for a reaction.

It takes effort to fight boredom. When people say, *I'm bored,* what they're really saying is, *I'm lazy.*

Ten minutes after I shut down the lemonade stand, I was mowing the snow with a lawn tractor. It's not a good way to move snow. Lawn tractors perform like shit in the snow – almost as bad as my Kia. So, I parked the tractor and moved on to the next thing.

The Ice Water Challenge in 2014 was funny because everyone who did it screamed like a colicky baby with a mousetrap on its toe. Cold water on warm skin will do that to you.

But that was a summer challenge, so I bet Michael I could do the same thing in the dead of winter. Specifically, the bet was that I could stand in the snow wearing nothing but shorts. Then, I'd dump a trash can filled with nasty grey slush over my head -- without making a peep.

He took the bet, so I drove the lawn tractor to the end of the driveway, where the plow left thick trails of sludgy, pebbly grey slush and slopped about twenty pounds of it into the trash can.

I wasn't allowed to make so much as a squeak when the slush hit my body. That was the bet. He recorded it, so a third party could review the audio in the event of a dispute.

The trash can was heavier than I thought, and when I dumped it over my head, the gritty slush crashed – yes, crashed – down on my skin like it came from a sandblaster.

It wasn't a good bet, for two reasons.

First, I misjudged the impact that the mixture of slush and small rocks would have on my body. It hurt. It was like getting hit with a wet porcupine... a dead, mushy one.

The other thing – I should have concentrated on keeping my mouth closed. That was my fault (unlike everything else, which was also my fault). At first, I thought all the fillings came out of my teeth, but then I realized they were just pebbles from the snow.

There was no need to review the tape. Once I spit the slush out of my mouth, I let out a shriek, and not an especially manly one. It was the sound of defeat.

At that point, I was officially cold, so I went inside and watched *Marriage Boot Camp.* Newlyweds were screaming at each other at the top of their lungs. He had sex with her best friend. She had sex with the minister who married them. He says she's a slut. She says he's gave one of her bridesmaids gonorrhea.

It's the show I claimed was proof that Americans are getting dumber. And yet, here I was, with pebbles in my mouth, recovering from a day of lemonade stands and riding the lawn mower in the snow and dumping slush on my head.

The difference is, *they* don't *know* they're being dumb.

FITNESS PEOPLE ARE ALWAYS talking about a body's muscle memory. The skin has memory too, and it was my skin's memory that kept me and my low tolerance for boredom inside the house for the rest of the winter. That was bad news for my favorite victim – Lisa.

I should really leave her alone when she's working from home. Of course, if I did everything I was supposed to do, I'd never do anything.

Lisa's got an excellent job as a Director for an international company. She also has her fitness business, and she was recently certified as a "Life Coach."

I am not a good advertisement for Lisa's life coaching business. People trust Lisa's expertise, guidance and advice – but they must wonder why it's not helping me.

It makes no sense. She's so professional, so grounded, so cultivated, so classy, so charming, so charismatic... and I saw him trying to lasso one of the statues in Crandall Park.

Lisa was in the middle of an important video conference call one evening around six o'clock. That's bad planning on Lisa's part because six o'clock is right around the time I require the most attention.

Once her call was underway, I grabbed my phone and took off all my clothes. I thought it would be funny to record her reaction when I dirty-danced my way into the room, totally naked.

Her only saving grace was that I couldn't find a bow, and not the kind that shoots arrows. I was going to gift wrap myself with it, and we all know where the bow goes -- on the package.

For me, everything like this needs to be a bet. For some reason, I think it justifies anything. This time, the bet was that she wouldn't be able to keep a straight face when I walked in the room and presented myself. Since there was no one else there, I made it a gentleman's bet with myself.

It was a video call, so I made sure the person on the other end wouldn't see me, although... how funny would that be?

Bam saw my naked body walking down the hall right toward him. He lifted his head and looked at me for about three seconds, then plopped it back down on his paws and went to sleep. I swear I saw him roll his eyes.

Now it was showtime. I waited till Lisa was in the middle of a sentence, then hopped into the room.

Tada!

She didn't even look at me.

I was just standing there, stark-naked, listening to her give advice to some woman about day planning. She didn't even know I was there.

I hopped again, but this time I made a high-pitched squeak.

She looked at me with the kind of expression people make when they discover dog poop on the carpet. It's not what I was going for. I was hoping for a little scream or a laugh. A simple acknowledgment would have been nice.

She stopped talking to the woman for a second, rubbed her forehead, then picked up right where she left off.

I stood there for a minute, wondering what went wrong. I decided it was the temperature that ruined my skit. It was too cold at the time, so my presentation wasn't as impressive as it could have been.

She should have at least giggled, not for me, but for herself – because now I was going back to the drawing board for something better.

LISA GOT HER PAYBACK as I was heading back to our bedroom. I was walking by one of her prized pets when it reached out and bit me – hard – right on the tip of my big toe.

A couple years earlier, when I returned to the lake house after leaving rehab, the first thing I noticed was that my vacuum cleaner was parked exactly where I left it when, apparently, I got pissed off and stopped vacuuming... forever.

I assumed that's what happened since the cord was running across the floor, and the plug was lying about three feet from the outlet.

Obviously, I pushed the vacuum too far and accidentally yanked the plug out of the wall for the millionth and final time. When you yank it out like that, based on my experience, the plug will travel about three feet.

Judging by the layer of dirt and dog hair on the carpet, I estimated that the vacuum was parked right where I found it for about a year.

In that final year, I was simply too fatigued from around-the-clock drinking to deal with the stress of plugging it back in – yes, stress.

I had long-since abandoned the whole concept of vacuuming the lake house floors. I couldn't go that long without a drink, and I was too unstable to maneuver a vacuum cleaner with one hand while holding a beer in the other.

There was so much Bam hair on the carpet, if I dropped a quarter on the floor, I might not find it again. Whenever I spilled a beer, Bam's thick shroud of hair soaked it up like a wool sweater. After that, there'd be beer-drenched dog hair on the floor, producing an unusual stench, like a pack of wolves having a keg party.

Of course, the vacuum cleaner, being in the middle of the floor like that, was in plain sight all day as I laid on the couch with my beer and vodka. It became a source of shame, a constant reminder of how hard I had fallen.

Today, vacuum cleaners continue to wreak havoc on my life. My wife has a fleet of them – Hoover, Dyson, Oreck, Shop Vac, Electrolux. If it sucks, she has it.

They're hanging in closets, hiding behind doors, and double-parked in hallways. On top of all that, our house has a built-in vacuum system. It has the sucking power of... it has a lot of sucking power.

There's only one vacuum she doesn't have yet, but we will.

It's just a matter of time before one of those voice-controlled, hockey pucks is sliding around the house – and it'll be just a matter of seconds before Bam pounces on the thing and rips it into a million tiny pieces.

Then again, at least the robot vacuums return to their little docking stations.

Lisa does what I used to do: she leaves them right where they are when she gets tired of vacuuming. At least once a week, I run into one her "prized pets" with my bare foot -- letting out a holy howl that wakes up Lisa and probably the neighbors.

I'd prefer to get bitten by a real pet. At least then, I could send it to bed without a bone. If I did anything to hurt one of Lisa's prized vacuums, I'd be the one without a bone.

This time, my collision with the vacuum caused extra trauma to my hallux metatarsal phalangeal, and my yelp was loud enough to get a reaction from Lisa.

"What's wrong honey. Are you okay?"

"I just jammed my toe on the fucking vacuum cleaner."

"Which one?"

"It was a blue Hoover Wind Tunnel bagless upright with dual suction, but I'm not sure which one. I didn't get the plate number."

I didn't really say that.

I'm the malcontent in our marriage. For every misdemeanor I accuse her of, she could throw ten felonies back at me. She can even write a book about it. Till then, I'd like to discuss the way she rakes leaves.

For starters, she doesn't even have to rake because I mulch the leaves with the mower. She just does it to get out of the house.

Every so often, she goes out there and does the same the same thing with leaves that she does with vacuum cleaners. She abandons them mid-chore. She likes making piles and waving at the neighbors, but then she just stops and leaves them there like hay bales in a pasture.

The least she could do is tell me to pick them up. Here's what she has to say about that:

"If you can't see that the leaves need to be picked up, I'll just pick them up the next time I'm doing yardwork."

Every man in the world knows what that means. It means: *Pick up the fucking leaves, you lazy prick. I shouldn't have to ask.*

I get it. Problem is, if I don't notice the piles right away and scoop them all up, the grass turns white, then dries up overnight and turns light brown. The next day, it looks like little flying saucers landed all over the yard. We're the only house on our block with crop circles.

Vacuum cleaners and crop circles, that's it. I can't think of anything else I'd change about her. I'm not sure I'd even change those things. I need *something* to complain about.

I've found the one person in this world who needs me as much as I need her. Whenever I feel like I need to see or talk to someone, it's always the best friend I have, my wife.

It would take a lot of writers a thousand words to segue from the last sentence to the next chapter. I'll do it in one: WARNING.

Chapter Fifteen

The Gross Glory of Reaching Out

THREE AND A HALF YEARS SOBER

I've seen my own semen, obviously... yes, obviously. All guys have seen their semen. In fact, they see it more often than they'd like to, and certainly more often than they'll admit. But it took me fifty-one years of walking around this earth before I saw another man's semen. That sounded awful. The whole thing sounds awful. I'll back up.

My friend Connor has been in and out of AA long enough to know about "stinking thinking." When you first get sober, you can't trust your own thoughts. You're going to be unstable for a week, month, year or, in my case, forever.

That's one of the reasons people in AA have sponsors. Especially in early recovery, they'll keep you grounded and on-track. If they're doing their job, they'll tell you when you're not thinking straight.

My friend Connor was just coming back to AA after falling off the wagon (and his Harley) during a weeklong bender. When I first met him, he reminded me of my brother – stubborn and rough around the edges -- so I made a point of checking in with him every so often.

We were talking about his relationship issues one day when I sensed that his thinking was off. He was jumping to conclusions about his girlfriend and letting his suspicions get the best of him. He seemed to be tiptoeing off the reservation.

A line from my first book seemed pertinent, so I repeated it to him:

"You know, not everything that crosses your mind is true."

Connor seemed to comprehend what I was saying.

"What, you think I'm fucked up?" he asked.

"No, but I think your thoughts are. Mine were too for a while. The next time you have a fucked-up thought, just text me. If your thinking sounds crazy, I'll tell you."

It's not that he was crazy, and I was sane. In fact, it's probably the other way around. It's just that, in certain situations, people in early sobriety should get the opinion of someone who's been off booze long enough to have a clear head.

Two nights later, I got a text from Connor.

"Okay, I'm gonna send you a picture. Look at it and tell me if I'm crazy."

The picture he sent was reminiscent of Monica Lewinski's infamous blue dress, the one stained with Bill Clinton's... um, trouser gravy.

"What does that look like to you?" he asked.

"It looks like semen, why?"

"Are you sure?" he asked.

A semen stain has a distinct appearance. It's hard to mistake for anything else. Still, I shouldn't have blurted out "SEMEN!" the second I saw it. I should have asked for a little background information, like where the stain was and why he was wondering about it.

"You don't think it could be anything else," he asked.

I tried stalling him while I Googled images for semen stains, something I never imagined I'd do – and, trust me, I deleted my search history as soon as I was done.

Every image I saw looked like Connor's… sample. The problem is, it wasn't Connor's. It was on the back of his girlfriend's sweater when she got home from work and, according to him, there was no way it could be his.

I started backtracking.

"Yeah, there's a million other things it could be."

Now I was Googling, "things that look like semen."

I never realized how many things looked like semen. I'll tell you one thing: I'm never eating partially cooked egg whites or sour cream again. Colgate toothpaste, really? Then there was dog slobber and, my favorite, donut glaze.

I texted him back. "Does she know anyone with a Saint Bernard?"

An alcoholic's brain is an unreliable source of information. It doesn't matter whether you've been sober for four days like Connor, four years like me, or four score and seven years ago like no one, an alcoholic's brain is inherently defective.

My friend Chad, who has the looks and demeanor of Ben Cartwright, likes to say, "My brain is broke; I try not to use it."

Connor did the right thing by calling me, especially since I told him he could. This time, unfortunately, instead of helping him with my clear mind, I reverted to my old alcoholic thinking and dove into the gutter with him.

"Go have sex with that chick from the Thursday meeting that likes you."

Hence, I doubled his thinking problem, because the only thing worse than one alcohol brain is two alcoholic brains.

"I want to be positive first," he said.

"I got an idea," I said.

Correction: The only thing worse than one alcoholic brain is when two alcoholic brains get together and start brainstorming.

Both of our alcoholic brains got online and found the same thing: semen test kits.

Apparently, there's a lot of paranoid men out there. I found a kit called, "Semen Spy." (Semen kits? Did we give up on curing cancer?)

Connor found a more dignified brand, which isn't to suggest there's a dignified way to investigate someone else's Twinkie filling.

He ordered a kit called "Check Mate," and it arrived in the mail about a week later. I saw him at a meeting that night.

"It came back negative," he said.

I wasn't sure what to say. Congratulations maybe?

"Oh, that's good, so... does she know you tested it?"

"Oh yeah, we did it together."

"Aww, you darling little lovebirds."

"Yeah, we're totally cool now."

I wanted to say, "Awesome sauce," but maybe it was too soon for that.

The meeting started. When the chairperson asked if there were any announcements, I looked at Connor.

I'm John and I'm an alcoholic. I just want to announce that the gook on Connor's girlfriend's sweater tested negative for semen. Let's give him a hand.

Too soon for that too.

The moral of the story is... well, there's two morals: One, a lot of things look like semen and, apparently, Connor's girlfriend was rolling around in at least one of them. Two, the mind isn't always a terrible thing to waste; sometimes it's a great thing to waste and a terrible thing to use.

CONNOR FELT COMFORTABLE coming to me about his sticky situation *(that's the last one)* because he'd read *You Can't Die: A Day of Clarity* and concluded that nothing could make the author blush.

Given my outstanding leadership throughout the semen crisis, several months later, I became Connor's sponsor, and he became my first and only sponsee. It's not necessarily what he wanted; it just worked out that way.

For the past four years, I've heard old-timers talk about "how it used to be" back in the rough and tumble days of Alcoholics Anonymous. I don't begrudge them one bit for romanticizing the "old days of the program" a little. If I'm still around in thirty years, I'll be doing the same thing.

Our grandparents used to talk about walking to school in four feet of snow – "and it was uphill both ways." Old-timers in AA like to talk about their drill sergeant sponsors and the hard life of early Alcoholics Anonymous. A sample:

"When I first came into the rooms, they told me to sit down and shut up. They'd say, 'Take the cotton out of your mouth and put it in your ears.' And after my first meeting, old man Jimmy Beam came up to me and said, 'Hey kid, Who's your sponsor?' I said I didn't have a sponsor and he said, 'From now on, I'm your sponsor. Now get over to my farm and plow my fields while balancing the Big Book of Alcoholics Anonymous on your head.' That's the way it was done back then. And we liked it because we stayed sober."

I may have dressed that up a bit, but not much.

When Connor reached his ninetieth day of sobriety, someone told him he was eligible to chair his first meeting, then asked him to do it one Monday night in Hudson Falls.

He didn't want to, of course. No one with only three months in the program wants to sit in front of a large group of people and pretend to know what they're doing. But, when you're asked, it's a good idea to say yes.

I was sitting in the back of the room with my sponsor, Vick R.

"Is this the first time Connor has chaired a meeting?" I asked him.

Vick R. nodded.

"If there's a long silence when he asks for a topic, I'll speak up, so he doesn't have to sit up there wondering what to do."

"Make sponsorship the topic," Vick R. said. "He needs one, and it might be time for you to have a sponsee."

"Am I ready for that?"

"I don't know, are you?"

I hate when he does that… making me think for myself, that is.

"A few times, I thought he was going to ask me," I said. "Maybe I'll just *tell* him I'm his sponsor."

Vick R. laughed.

"You could do that."

I hate when he does that, too. I knew I *could* do it. I could also shave my balls with a blow torch. It doesn't make it a good idea.

But I get it. He wouldn't have suggested it if he didn't think I was ready. With Vick R., it's always a suggestion, not an order. Alcoholics don't take orders anyway; they do the opposite of what they're ordered to do.

The meeting got underway, and Connor was doing a decent job in front of the big group. He asked for a topic and someone else suggested one before I could get my hand up.

About halfway through the meeting, there was a few seconds of silence because no one was volunteering to share. Connor looked at me. I stuck my tongue out at him.

"John?"

"You're calling on me?"

"Yeah."

"Okay, you might regret it. I'm John and I'm an alcoholic."

I said a few things about the importance of having a sponsor, then admonished him a little for not having one. It was bad AA etiquette on my part, but my etiquette is bad everywhere. It's not like it improves when I walk through the doors of AA.

Besides, I was just trying to gauge his reaction before putting him on the spot in front of a full meeting. I was firing a warning shot.

"You need a sponsor," I said, while glaring at him and tugging at the back of my sweatshirt, hoping he would realize I was dropping a hint about his girlfriend's sweater.

That was my way of sending him a message.

When I tell you I'm your sponsor, you better pretend to be happy about it, or else I'll tell everyone about your girlfriend's nasty sweater.

It was a bluff; I'd never do that. I waited for an indication that he got the drift.

His fake smile said, "Yes." His rapid head-nodding said, "What the fuck are you doing to me?"

With that, I was confident he got the message, so I threw it out there.

"From now on I'm your sponsor."

There was laughter when I told him he had to call me every day, but I also noticed one or two looks of disapproval for putting him on the spot while he was chairing a meeting.

Really, you hypocrites? Aren't you constantly bragging about your sponsors doing the same thing to you in 1912, before AA was even around?

Whatever. Thirty years from now, Connor will be saying:

When I came into the program in 2017, old John W. waited till I was chairing a meeting and then he rushed up to the table and smashed my hand with the gavel until I begged him to be my sponsor. That's the way we did it back then -- and we liked it because it kept us sober.

IF I HADN'T WRITTEN my first book, I never would have known the glory of helping Connor remove the stain of suspicion *(just one more after this)* from his life.

Originally, I had planned on keeping my AA friends in the dark about the book. In theory, they could read the book without knowing I was the author, but it's a theory built on another theory – a faulty one – that last names are anonymous in AA.

These days, you can type a few things into a search engine and have a person's DNA in the palm of your hand. Just ask Connor. *(That's it. Done.)*

I'm not sure how the book spilled into the rooms, but it took less than a day for it to happen. Keeping it out was a plan that was doomed for failure, and I don't remember what my rationale for secrecy was in the first place.

Something told me that the book would affect my AA relationships. Part of me worried that I was violating one of AA's Twelve Traditions.

To be sure I wasn't, I gave an early copy to JR, just to gauge his reaction. JR has been in the program since I was in high school, which is probably when I should have started coming in. He's no AA Nazi, but he's serious enough about the program to throw the flag when its traditions are being compromised, which is good. *Someone* has to do it.

At a Schuylerville meeting one night, some guy was going on ad infinitum about a new herbal drug and how smoking it consistently sent him into a blissful trance while listening to the "second guitar solo" of some Pink Floyd song.

It went on for a long time, long enough to get top billing on my list of most cringeworthy moments in AA.

JR didn't cut him off. At the appropriate time, he tactfully reminded everyone one that Alcoholics Anonymous is for alcoholics and Narcotics Anonymous is for addicts – and although both programs welcome members from the other, neither program is a place to glorify... whatever this idiot was glorifying.

If there was something detrimental to AA in the first book, JR wouldn't have been shy about pointing it out to me. When he was halfway through, he said he couldn't put it down. When he was done, it was clear I had nothing to worry about.

The other concern I had – and still have – was using my disease and my misadventures to sell books. I didn't like the idea of wrapping my horrendous experience in a colorful, glossy book cover. That fear was exacerbated when the main title was unavoidably changed from "A Day of Clarity" to "You Can't Die."

"You can't Die" became the title because of a registration error at Amazon that couldn't be corrected without confusing people who ordered the book early.

"You Can't Die" was simply intended to be a floating quote on the front cover, not the title.

The line was pulled from an email my mother sent me when I was circling the drain. Outside of that context, the title sounds histrionic… like something hatched up by the headline writers at the *New York Post.*

My mom's email was only piece of the story behind "You Can't Die." I deleted the other two pieces, including a mention of Bam, which was a shitty way to repay him for his unconditional love.

When I first got my mom's email in August of 2013, I stopped reading as soon as I got to "You can't die." At that point, I was pretty sure I was going to die, and the last thing I needed was my mother telling me that I wasn't allowed to.

When I closed out of my email tab, YouTube was on the screen. It was playing random songs off some generic playlist that been running all day, along with the TV.

After passing out for a while, I woke up and started drinking again, trying to recover the buzz I lost by passing out. As usual, I gulped vodka while staring at whatever was on the computer screen. After each gulp, I'd rest my chin on my hands while waiting for the vodka to reach my brain.

On this day, just hours after I got my mom's email, a song by some group called the "New Radicals" was playing karaoke-style, with the lyrics scrolling in big letters across the screen. I looked up once and saw the words, "You're in harm's way," then did a doubletake and saw, "Can't die."

Bam was right there, as usual, with his chin resting on my leg.

I used to talk to Bam a lot in those days. I still talk to him now, but I don't have full conversations with him like I used to. Also, when I talked to Bam back then, I would say something, then wait for an answer. I don't do that anymore.

After reading my mom's email, then seeing similar words on the computer screen, I was freaked out. I wasn't scared; I was sad.

"That's twice today someone has told me not to die, Bam."

I sat there for a long time, staring at Bam, looking for a glimmer of... something. He loved me, and that was all I needed to get through the rest of that day.

A LOT OF AA PEOPLE couldn't reconcile the guy they knew from the meeting with the guy in the book. A few didn't even believe the picture of me in the book was really me.

At a meeting, George, who has a fetish for showing people pictures on his phone, was flashing a picture of me from 2002 -- the same picture on the back cover of the book.

He showed it to Wayne and Mary Lynne, a married couple in the program. She looked at it, then looked up at me and shook her head.

"That's not you."

I had no idea what she was looking at. For all knew, George was showing her a picture of Luke Skywalker. It was me standing at a podium, looking over a speech in the State Assembly Chamber.

"Yeah, that's me."

"No," she said.

It's hard to argue with that. In the picture, I was better looking, clean cut, serious and dressed in a suit. On the outside, I was impeccable. On the inside, I was a disaster.

Today, I'm a disaster on the outside. On the inside, I'm... well, I suppose the jury is still deliberating, but I'm not a disast... like I said, the jury is still deliberating.

MY BOOK PAGE ON FACEBOOK was flooded with messages after the book came out. Most of them were from people I didn't know who identified with my story on some level. I got a few messages from people who crossed paths with me during my long blackout period up at the lake house.

One woman said they read the book, loved it, and had a favor to ask. She wanted me to reach out to a young person struggling with alcoholism.

"Of course," I told her.

It was postscript to her message that really grabbed my attention:

"I don't know if you remember me, but we meet at Loon lake during your darker days."

Here we go.

I assumed I'd be writing either an apology or a child support check before the conversation was over. I decided to get that part of the discussion out of the way.

"Do I owe you an apology? My twelve years in Chestertown are a blur."

"I rented a place on the lake. We were trying to figure out what was wrong with you. Honestly, at first, we thought you had a head injury, but finally concluded you were just super wasted."

It was a little of both, actually. A brain can go without oxygen for ten minutes, but some brains need all the air they can get – and mine went without it for over a minute. It's still trying to catch its breath.

The good news is we didn't have sex. Rarely is that good news but, after five years, it would be a little late to enjoy it.

She mailed me a copy of my book and asked me to write a note to the young person she was trying to help. Helping another alcoholic is one of the few unselfish things I'll do all day, every day, without feeling burdened. It helps me stay sober and hopefully it will help them *get* sober.

I must admit, though, that helping other alcoholics wasn't the original intent of the book. The book was my way of coming clean about everything -- confessing, explaining, apologizing and seeking absolution.

In AA, comparing your experience to the experience of others is generally discouraged. That's impossible. It's only by comparing our rock bottom to others that we appreciate how far down the scale we fell.

In terms of raw, physical addiction to alcohol, I've only met one person in AA who drank as much as I did just to fight the symptoms of withdrawal. He and I share a rock bottom that is more common in intensive care units and cemeteries than it is in the rooms of AA.

And, because that's the case, my story could have the deleterious effect of enabling alcoholics looking to downplay their own drinking. My story could easily convince an alcoholic that he or she don't have a problem.

If a person drinks a twelve-pack every day, they might walk away from my book thinking they're a social drinker.

Compared to me, they probably are. Compared to the rest of the world, they're an alcoholic. But, aside from my people like my mother, who has the temerity (mom doesn't have balls) to tell them that?

Several people implied that they were worried about their drinking until they read my book. That's not good. One guy said that the book would help him convince his family that he didn't have a problem. That's even worse than not good.

As plainly as I could, I told him not to think that way. Then, I wrote a general response to anyone who made that inference.

"Don't stop worrying on my account. I'm a bad yardstick to use to measure your drinking. My book is a dream come true for people in denial. Every sentence of it can be used to fend off a concerned family member or an intervention. If you use it that way, you've missed the point. Your drinking may not be as bad as mine was. Give it time. If your family is upset about your drinking, it means your drinking is hurting them. That, right there, means you have a problem."

It's not warm and fuzzy, but that's the message that resonated loudest with me.

I'm no alcohol counselor. There's probably a softer way to carry the message. I'm just not sure that softer is better.

I never heard from the first guy again. Mostly likely, he's still out there, trying to prove his family wrong.

The book had a better effect on a few people who read it and got scared they were heading down the same path. One message came from an old friend I hadn't seen in over ten years. I had no idea he had a problem with drinking.

"I tried taking a day off [from drinking]," he said. "I can't even do that."

"I can research the rehabs in your area. Will you go?" I asked.

"That's what I wanted to ask you. What's rehab like?"

"You'll love it. Why do you think I kept going back?"

He wanted to know if rehab was like a twenty-eight-day AA meeting. If it was, he didn't think he could handle the boredom.

"I went to an AA meeting," he said. "There were a lot of odd ducks in there talking about meaningless stuff."

"Odder than the ducks you hung out with in bars? What meaningful conversations did you have with those people?"

We texted back and forth for a long time after that. He continued to drink, but he managed to stay sober long enough to attend two or three AA meetings.

"I still feel uncomfortable in those meetings," he told me.

It's hard to sit through an AA meeting when there's alcohol waiting for you in the car.

When you're drunk, everyone is smart, good-looking and funny. When you're craving alcohol, they're all motherfucking cunts. Pardon the forbidden words, but nothing else can convey the pure, irrational hatred that flows through the blood of a craving alcoholic.

Six months later, my old friend checked into a rehab, and came out feeling the way a lot of people do when they're clearheaded for the first time in years. He was high-spirited, energetic and gung-ho about sobriety -- riding the euphoria of early sobriety, which is great, but it doesn't always last forever.

"I wish I could take pictures at the meetings I go to," he told me. "We have a blast."

"Glad you're having fun, but don't do that."

The euphoria he was feeling is called a "pink cloud." It may last a month or a year. I hope his lasts forever. When this book went to print, he was still sober, going to meetings and riding high on the pink cloud.

A LOT OF ALCOHOLICS need to get beaten down before they address their drinking. They need to see the ominous red glow rising from the black sky.

The red glow isn't some myth. Millions of people have seen it while driving at night. Some have been sucked into it, never to be seen again. It's altogether fitting that the red glow looks like the gates to hell. If you've been drinking, it usually is.

I started driving in 1983, but I didn't drive into a DWI checkpoint until 2016 – thirty-three years later. I drove into another one in 2017. Both times I was on my way to an AA meeting. Props to my Higher Power.

It was pitch dark outside when I saw the infamous red glow for the first time. I was in Glens Falls, heading to a meeting in Hudson Falls when it appeared on the horizon.

The next thing I saw was an unmarked black police car on the side of the road, right before a sharp turn.

Once you see that, it's obvious what's causing the beautiful red glow in the distance, but it's too late to do a U-turn. He'll chase you down and bring your ass right back to the nightmare that awaits you around the corner.

I knew what was around the corner, and even though I'd been sober for three years, I was worried.

Believe it or not, I had this thought:

What if my liver puffs out one last breath of alcohol?

There was a line of traffic cones and cops with little flashlights.

I rolled down the window as I pulled up to first one.

He waved me forward, pointing further down a line of about six officers.

"Go right down the line until you get to my sergeant"

Until I get to your sergeant? Is that part of the test?

Most people can't tell the difference between a sergeant and a four-star general. I wasn't sure if I could either. There were five officers in the line and only one without a badge on his hat. I figured that was Sarge.

He flashed his light at my registration and inspection stickers.

"Good evening. Everything looks good here. So, you're out celebrating tonight?"

Celebrating what, Hump Day? It's just another Wednesday.

"No, I'm just heading out to a... thing with friends."

I didn't say I was going to an AA meeting because I didn't want to raise a red flag. Going to an AA meeting means you're an alcoholic trying to get better. It doesn't necessarily mean you're sober.

Of course, going to a "thing with friends" isn't much better.

He leaned in a little closer with his light.

"Thanks for driving safely. Have a good night."

That was it. He just walked away.

I was floored. For three decades, my worst fear was driving into a DWI checkpoint. It's the reason I didn't drink and drive... very much. If I had known that getting through a checkpoint was as easy as driving through a car wash, I probably would have driven drunk more often.

I drove away from the checkpoint thinking the cops weren't doing their jobs. Even after twenty beers, I could have acted just as sober as I did for the Sarge. I wondered why they were being so lax. Turns out, they weren't.

About eighteen months later, on the evening before Thanksgiving, I was driving to a meeting in Fort Edward when another beautiful red glow appeared above the trees in the distance.

A few seconds later, there was a big yellow sign on the side of the road. It said, "Sobriety Checkpoint," and right behind it, of course, was an unmarked police car, waiting for the first drunk driver dumb enough to do a U-turn.

I decided it was a good time to make a funny video. I grabbed my phone and started recording while narrating and driving. After fifteen seconds, I still hadn't said anything funny, but I figured I'd think of something good when I got to the officers.

I was about thirty feet from the first officer when it realized what I was doing – aiming a camera at a group of cops while driving toward them. That's a six-pointer in New York State.

I threw the phone on the seat, rolled down my window and prayed they didn't write me up for being a distracted douchebag.

Either they didn't see the phone, or they didn't care.

It was the same drill as before. The first officer told me to pull up to another one near the end of the line. The second officer walked up with his little flashlight.

"How are you doing tonight, Sir?"

"Pretty good," I said. "No drinking, no drugs."

"Wonderful. Have a good night."

What the fuck?

Just like before, there was no scrutiny -- no probing questions, no light in my eye, no checking my license, or registration or proof of insurance. He was there for barely a second before waving me through and walking on to the next car.

Again, all I could think about was how easily I could have gotten past this checkpoint when I was drinking.

This time was even easier than the last. I figured I could have breezed through this one with a bottle of vodka between my legs, a beer in the cup holder, and a joint behind my ear.

At least, that's what I thought until I was talking to a cop friend a few days later.

"Yeah," I told him. "They barely even looked at me before waving me through. It was kind of a joke."

"It probably seemed that way, but I guarantee they got everyone who was drinking," he said.

"The cop who talked to me didn't even lean in to smell my breath."

"Did he have a little flashlight?"

"Yeah, a weird little thing with red stripes... wait, you've gotta be shitting me!"

"It's called a Passive Alcohol Sensor," he said. "He knew you weren't drinking the second you rolled down your window."

I'm sure they consider their beer-sniffing flashlight cutting edge technology, but my mother had something better than that thirty years ago: her nose. I could gargle with perfume and Drain-o and she'd still pick up the scent of a beer from twenty feet away.

A week earlier, Vick R., my sponsor, told me to start working on a "Gratitude List." That night, I drove away with something to put at the top of the list. Thank God they didn't have that little flashlight when I was drinking.

Chapter Sixteen

The Politics of Not Drinking

ALMOST FOUR YEARS SOBER

The "Class of 2013" is probably the hokiest thing I've ever come up with, which is why I haven't shared it with anyone until now. It's just a way of referring to a handful of friends in AA who got sober the same year as me. We're all about the same age – within five years – and we're all "low bottom drunks," meaning we had a high tolerance for misery and needed to hit rock bottom before getting better.

It's never uplifting when another person relapses. It happens all the time and you must accept that, as Chad likes to say, you're not God. But, when a person who reminds you of yourself relapses, it's scary.

Mitch came into the program a month before me. Two days after he celebrated his third year of sobriety, the Class of 2013 got smaller when he went out and celebrated again, this time with a bottle of scotch.

He was always talking about a liquor store he had to pass every afternoon.

"Some days, that neon sign at the front of the store is just calling out my name."

If I were in the same situation, hopefully I'd have taken a different route home. Maybe I'd have pushed the visor over to block my view of the store.

In driver's ed., they told us that, when an oncoming car has its high beams on, you should look at the solid white line on the right side of the road. Maybe that's the tactic he should have used to avoid seeing the sign.

I wonder about these things on purpose, to prevent the same thing from happening to me. I need to ask, "Is there a four-year curse that I should worry about, or did he just screw up?"

The answer is simple. He just screwed up.

Neon signs aren't a trigger for me, but he knew they were a trigger for him and he did nothing to avoid the one that was "calling his name."

He was also going to about one meeting a week, which means that, six days a week, he was passing that sign without a headful of AA. He was hearing one side of a debate about booze, and the neon sign was winning six to one. It was just a matter of time.

It's easy to scrutinize his mistakes, but what about my own?

Right around the time I celebrated my three-year anniversary, I started looking at my own vulnerabilities. The timing couldn't have been better, because it was a presidential election year — a really fucked up presidential election year.

This was the first election in my lifetime where no one was apathetic. Everyone had an opinion, and nine out of ten times, it was a nasty opinion articulated with a lot of screaming and four-letter words.

One reporter interviewed a shirtless dude who was rioting in the streets of Oakland. Not only did he have an opinion, it was an informed opinion. He said he was hoping for "a stronger third-party candidate."

I swear this guy was packing a Mack 10 – but he was displeased with the field of candidates?

I had to stay out of it entirely. For me, working in politics wasn't like football -- it hadn't been good to me. Instead, it has always brought out the worst in me.

POLITICS ISN'T HIGH on the list of reasons people relapse.

Most treatment counselors and AA sponsors agree that relationships top the list. They say that alcoholics and addicts in early recovery should refrain from making big decisions in their first year of sobriety.

I broke that rule in the first six months by getting married to Lisa and moving to South Glens Falls, even though both decisions were an immediate, happy success.

Some hardline sponsors insist on no sex for the first year. I broke that rule in three hours and that was an even happier and more immediate success, which is probably more than you needed to know.

My second roommate at St. Mary's abstained from sex every morning, but only until I left the room. Unfortunately for him, rehab rules prohibit locking doors, and the nurses frequently walked in unannounced.

Sex was never a trigger for me. Don't get me wrong: I've had my share of regrettable bedmates. I drank to get into them, then I drank to forget them, and they probably drank to forget whatever sloppy, freakish fetish I talked them into.

These days, and probably for the last twenty years, my trigger is the toxic world of politics that once dominated my life.

Thank God I finished rehab in 2013 instead of 2016. If I had walked out of the hospital to the election of 2016, I'd have gone straight to the nearest liquor store. I realize that's not much of a statement since I always went to the liquor store after rehab but, in 2016, the politics would have driven me there.

It's hard to be a good politician and a good person at the same time. Politics brings out the worst in people, especially politicians who used to be honest, decent people.

I've worked for three elected executives – Monroe County Executives Robert L. King and Jack Doyle, and New York Governor George E. Pataki.

King and Pataki were two peas in a pod – brainy, idealistic and, in the beginning, above reproach.

Doyle, on the other hand, was a loud, confrontational former judge who liked his politics the way he liked his collaborators – dirty.

I liked Doyle the most -- not because he was crass, foulmouthed and dirty -- but because he was honest about it. Doyle didn't do anything more devious than Pataki and King wound up doing during their tenures. He was just less ashamed of it.

I wrote for all three of the guys. I sat with them at length. I knew what they wanted to say versus what they really thought. I quickly learned about the necessary evils of politics, and practiced it with my pen, day after day for over twenty years.

It didn't take me long to jump in the mud with the rest of the pigs. I went from idealistic to dirty in less than a year.

I'll use an early example to avoid feather ruffling and civil suits.

In 1994, there was a Rochester lawyer named Gene Welsh. He was running for the office of County Executive, an office with a constituency of about a million people.

At the time, I despised the guy... probably because I worked for the County Executive he was trying to unseat. If he won, I'd be out of a job. But for me, it got even more personal than that.

Welsh complained that his enemies were destroying his lawn signs. Unfortunately, sign stealing happens in every election. It's pathetic but whining about it is just as pathetic. Get over it.

Welsh also complained that the County Executive (my boss) had, "a professional, taxpayer-funded political writer." He was talking about me.

He was running a campaign against political cronyism, which is fine. What bothered me was his faux outrage, carrying on like Renault in Casablanca.

I am shocked – shocked -- to find that gambling is going on in here!

Welsh was shocked to learn there was politics in politics.

One night, King and Welsh were taking part in a moderated debate in front of about four hundred people. I was sitting near the front of the large room, minding my own business and taking advantage of the open bar.

I wasn't even paying attention until, out of the blue, I heard Welsh saying my name.

"That's him right there, isn't it, Mr. King? Why don't you stand for us, Mr. Wolfe, so people can see the public relations machine they're paying for."

It was one of those rare occasions where I exercised enough restraint to stay seated instead of jumping up and telling him to go fuck himself.

Every high elected official has political appointees. Calling them out by name is not okay, especially when it's me. Fortunately for everyone, the moderator stopped Welsh dead in his tracks, and that was the end of it. Wait, no it wasn't.

I once heard a guy say, "The best revenge is massive success." Fuck that. The best revenge is massive payback.

See what I mean about politics bringing out the worst in people?

The first thing I did was steal a bunch of his stupid lawn signs. Stealing lawn signs is petty and classless, but it was pissing him off and it made me feel better. When the scales tilt like that, I can tune out my morals for an hour or two.

I knew it would be a disaster if I got caught. Local media would have a field day if the "taxpayer-funded political hack" this guy complained about turned out to be something worse than that — like a taxpayer-funded sign-stealer.

I didn't take any chances. Dressed in all black, I drove to a dark commercial street where I'd seen a few of his signs and snatched three of them from one intersection.

The scuzzy act of taking the signs was, ironically, nothing more than an evil mind game to make him *think* everyone was stealing his signs. Getting the signs was just the button. What I did with them was the bomb.

For a bitter, insecure guy like Welsh, nothing is more wickedly-effective than a propaganda bomb. I went home and cut each sign into ten postcard-sized rectangles, stuck a stamp on the front of each one and wrote messages on the back.

I made them look exactly like real postcards. The front of them, of course, was the glossy side of his sign. It showed just enough of his blue and yellow political logo for him to recognize what it was.

The message on first postcard was fairly blunt: "Stop lying about my boss's record. Every time you do it, I'll send you another hundred postcards, and it takes ten of your lawn signs to make that many."

All of this, even for me, is bizarre and obsessive behavior.

I mailed them en masse from a dozen different postal boxes around the city. At first, I sent them to his house, until I realized other members of his family would likely see the messages before he did. That's a little too low, even by my standards, so I directed the rest of them to his campaign headquarters.

I tried imagining the looks on the faces his interns as they sifted through stacks of nasty postcards made from their boss's lawn signs.

It wasn't the kind of thing that would influence an election, nor was it meant to. But, it would absolutely turn an otherwise sane candidate into a fire-breathing lunatic.

Apparently, it freaked him out so much, he was afraid to complain about it publicly. Instead, he called the County Executive's Office and begged them to figure out who was doing it and ask them to stop.

Everyone assumed it was just some psychopath looking for attention. I stopped doing it as soon as I heard about the phone call, before anyone learned that the psychopath was me.

The only thing worse than being sleazy at the county level is being sleazy at the state level. I was sleazy at both levels. I'm just not dumb enough to publicize the *state* sleaze in a book.

I never even liked politics and I hated pandering... having to appeal to every demographic of the human species with a perpetual stream of sanctioned lying.

I don't care how well you write, it's impossible to write great bullshit, although the *New York Times* prides itself on it.

I'm ideological, not political. There used to be a meaningful distinction. I've read every presidential inaugural address at least once, and quite a few of the gubernatorial addresses. They stopped being eloquent in the 90s.

The legacy of visionary presidential rhetoric disappeared with the Internet. It's just a matter of time until every American receives the State of the Union in one giant Snapchat.

I liked the day-after-the-inaugural rhetoric, where you could speak from the heart without having to worry about an impending election.

I dreaded identity politics, when you change your message based on the ethnicity or race or religion or gender you're trying to target. Some people think of it as a science, and they love it. I hate those people. Maybe hate is too strong a word. I vehemently disli... no, hate is the right word.

Take all that hate, mix it with politics and a million gallons of booze, and you have all the ingredients for some vast toxic wasteland where I am king and only bad things happen.

Here's the long overdue point of all this. I've found that politics is a lot like drinking. When people are engaging in it, they get upset if you refuse to join them.

I can never return to the world of politics for the same reason I can never take painkillers. Neither one of them are alcohol, just like gas isn't fire, but put them together, and... you get the point. Thanks for waiting three pages for it.

By returning to politics, I don't mean *working* in politics. I mean working, talking, thinking, writing, watching, engaging... all those things. I'll vote, but that's all I'll do. Politics and drinking is a package deal, and AA has kept me a safe distance from both.

In fact, I witnessed a miracle in the rooms of AA on November 9th, 2016 – and it had nothing to do with a higher power.

Just hours after the most anticipated and contentious election in U.S. history, I went to my usual Wednesday morning AA meeting. There was a lot of talking and laughing as I walked in the door -- and not a word of it had anything to do with the election.

And that's the way it went for the next hour, as we talked and laughed about everything from relationships to relapses to character defects – everything but politics. No one uttered a word about the most sensational news story since OJ.

So, maybe it *was* a higher power.

The Tenth Tradition of AA is a brilliant piece of wisdom and, although it pertains to AA as an organization, not its individual members, I decided to make it my personal creed: *I have no opinion on outside issues; hence my name ought never be drawn into public controversy.*

It doesn't mean people in AA are apolitical or apathetic. It simply means they know where the line is drawn, and they don't cross it.

If California got hit with a massive earthquake that brought down the Millennium Tower, people would feel comfortable discussing it out loud at an AA meeting. It's not controversial. There should only be one opinion on it – it's tragic. Hopefully, no one would think it was funny.

I need that in my life. I need a line that keeps me on the safe side of recovery. In the first three years of my recovery, I crossed the line, and it took me too long to step back.

An alcoholic can turn any travesty into a good idea. If something is illegal, but an alcoholic wants to do it anyway, all he must do is shuffle the facts in his head a few times, play with the semantics a little and twist a truth or two. Before you know it, in the alcoholic's mind, it's legal.

I can't go to Tokyo and drink Sapporo. Hopefully, I could never convince myself that it's not technically drinking because I'm in Japan.

Yet, in 2016 and 2017, I convinced myself that it was okay to dig my nose into international politics because it was in, of all places, Israel.

That makes sense, right? I mean, it's not like there's any inflammatory issues over *there*.

I dove into the fray, not once, but seven times, in a series of published articles in the *Times of Israel*, excoriating the anti-Israel boycott movement.

I knew it was a bad idea. I justified it by drawing a distinction without a difference. In fact, I justified it in an early draft of this book, until reread it and laughed at myself for writing something I'd crucify someone else for writing. Here's what almost made it into this book:

"The difference between [politics in Israel] and conventional politics is that, in the civilized world, there's no one on the other side of the issue. There's certainly no one in my world on the other side of the issue, no matter where they fall on the mainstream political spectrum. Anyone outside of that spectrum, left or right, isn't worth worrying about."

Yeah, that's me talking. In other words, "I can write about Israeli politics because I'm right and anyone who doesn't agree with me is a lunatic."

These days, I don't even watch the news. I tune out everything with even a whiff of politics in it -- everything from broadcast news to Hollywood pontificating to Facebook debates.

I'm on a mission. I'm to develop an opinion on one thing and one thing only – nothing. I don't even watch shows whose politics I tend to agree with. I'll stick to *Law and Order* and *Modern Family*, two shows that are largely devoid of all things political.

If those aren't on, I go for the Weather Channel, and it's not because I care about the dewpoint in Glens Falls or the light and variable winds in Tampa. It's because, unless there's a tsunami heading for the lake house, there's not one thing a meteorologist can say to raise my blood pressure.

Sure, occasionally they'll mention climate change, which can be a politically-charged issue. Call me a selfish bastard, but I support climate. Just settle down, Subaru Outback drivers, and hear me out.

Climate change benefits me. If it's as bad as they say, the weather is going to be awesome in Glens falls during my golden years. That means I won't have a heart attack with a shovel in my hand. It's not the funny death I'm hoping for.

Thanks to climate change, when Mallory and Jackson retire, they'll be able to stay in New York instead of moving to Florida.

My grandchildren's grandchildren will be little warm, but they can keep moving north until it's time to head to Alaska and watch the glaciers melt.

After they're gone, I have no legacies to worry about and, therefore, no vested interest in earthly weather. It'll be hotter than Hell up there, which means it'll be slightly hotter than where I'll be.

Here's the other benefit of climate change: A million years from now, dinosaur fossils will be gone. If we humans are so concerned about the future, we need to look long into that future and do our part for tomorrow's archeologists.

We need to replenish dinosaur fossils with our own fossils. The only way to do that is if we, as an unselfish people, die off every so often.

When the next round of humans comes around, think of how happy they'll be when they discover their first human fossil. Maybe it'll be Harvey Weinstein and they won't be able to tell if it's a human, a Neanderthal or a woolly mammoth.

All the above proves my point.

The mere mention of politics several paragraphs back regressed to a gutter tirade that ended with an insult against a defenseless Hollywood producer who's no longer in a position of power. Now I'm the bully.

LOOKING BACK, SEVERAL pages back at this point, the whole political sign-postcard thing is funny but, when I did it, I wasn't trying to be funny, which makes it not funny.

I wasn't trying to be mean, either. I just lost my ability to look inward and reel myself in. It may have been the onset of manic behavior. I started drinking so much in the years that followed, no one ever noticed, or maybe they mistook angry and reckless for drunk.

Take the alcohol away from an alcoholic and it's not uncommon to find a nutcase. In early sobriety, I was constantly looking in the mirror to see if I had Jack Nicholson in *The Shining* looking back at me.

You can't rely on other people to break that kind of news to you. Lisa and my mother knew something was up, but they weren't going to tell me. They weren't about to hand me a reason to drink again. Instead, they went behind my back and called Dr. Stiller. The women in my life are smarter than the man in theirs.

Based on the information fed to him by my two den mothers, Dr. Stiller jotted a couple things down, grabbed a big beaker and some test tubes and returned to his laboratory.

He crushed up a little of this, and mixed it with a little of that, shook up some potions, stirred it all together, then screamed, "Eureka!" and wrote a secret note to the man in the white uniform at Rite Aid.

"Just go hand this piece of paper to the nice man at the back of the store."

That's what I did, and the next day, everything made sense again.

It was just like the last time Dr. Stiller adjusted my pharmaceutical diet. Both times, I was treated to a day of clarity.

On paper, that means I'm crazy.

My sponsor talks about "staying in your own two-foot square." It's a polite way of saying mind your own fucking business. As soon as this book is done, I'm going to do that.

If I'm crazy, what's the diagnosis of people who seem crazy to *me?* Are they double crazy? Or are they the opposite of me, meaning perfectly sane?

I was behind this woman in Target. She was in the process of paying and I just finished putting all my stuff on the conveyor thing. When the cashier was done ringing her up, she objected to the way some of her items rang up.

"There was a sign saying this was twenty five percent off."

The cashier told the woman that you need an app on your phone to get the discount.

So, the woman digs into her purse for a phone and decides that this would be a good time to learn how to use it. The cashier is giving her instructions on how to type in Target's website.

After a few minutes -- and I am not making this up -- she said her phone was dying and asked if she could plug it into an outlet.

Then, the person behind me steps up to the plate.

"Here," she said, handing the cashier her phone. "I have the discount app. You can scan mine for her."

"Thanks," said the cashier.

The ungrateful woman said nothing... except this:

"So, I'll get the discount now?"

"Yes."

"But wait, then I won't get the points!" -- points she didn't even know existed five minutes earlier.

This woman is roaming the streets free, and I'm crazy? Let me tell you about crazy...

Chapter Seventeen

Cars Don't Drive People Crazy, People Drive People Crazy

FOUR YEARS SOBER

Most people are crazy. I'll prove that by the time I'm done here.

The shrinks should put away their ink blots and make their patients drive through a rotary. Everything you need to diagnose a person can be learned by watching how they do it. With few exceptions, people go through rotary's the same way they go through life.

There are five kinds of rotary drivers. Here are their street names, character defects, symptomatic behaviors and diagnoses.

1) *The fake-stopper is untrustworthy.* This is the guy who's trying to merge into the rotary. He stops, then goes a couple feet, then stops again, then drives another couple feet, making everyone in the rotary slam on their brakes because it looks like he's going to pull out in front of them. The fake-stopper typically suffers from **premature ejaculation**.

2) **The bully drives a Dodge Challenger.** *He's insecure about his sexuality.* This guy does the same thing as the fake stopper, but he does it on purpose, to reinforce his masculinity. He lurches forward, trying to scare people into slamming on their brakes so he can shove his way in. The bully has **inadequacy** issues and, in most cases, a small penis.

3) **The people-pleaser drives a minivan.** *He can't make a move by himself.* This friendly fellow drives through the rotary slowly, occasionally stopping and waving another car in. He's so focused on pleasing the drivers in front of him, he doesn't realize he's destroying the lives of the drivers behind him. Yeah, the crowd-pleaser is a textbook **codependent.**

4) **The straight man drives an Oldsmobile.** He thinks the rotary is a square instead of a circle. He drives in straight lines, giving you no indication of where in the fuck he's going. This guy doesn't even try to hide it. He just hates gays **(homophobe).**

5) **The bulldozer drives a Dodge Ram that's jacked up way too high.** He's an undisputed asshole and doesn't even pause before jumping on the rotary. He just drives no matter what's in front of him, knowing everyone else will get out of his way. You can find this deviant on your state's sex registry. Invariably, he is a **Level 3 sexual offender.**

Psychobabble aside, isn't the diagnosis for all five drivers the same? Aren't they all assholes? Isn't that how we diagnose them on the street?

Some reader may be thinking, "Not me. I'm a good driver." Trust me, someone out there thinks you drive like an asshole.

Case in point:

You're on a country road. The speed limit is 55 miles per hour, and that's how fast you want to go. The guy in front of you is going 50 mph.

You think he's an asshole for going too slow. He thinks you're an asshole for following too closely. And the guy behind you thinks you're an asshole for not passing.

Let's break this down. You think everyone else in this scenario is an asshole, but everyone else thinks you're the asshole. That's two asshole votes for you and only one for each of them. By a margin of two to one, you're the biggest asshole on that country road.... and yet, you're the one who's driving the speed limit.

Here's how the rest of my study shakes out. After driving through the rotary in Glens Falls twice a day for four years, I predict that forty nine percent of the population drives through a rotary just fine. The other fifty one percent doesn't. They fall into at least one of my five rotary categories.

That proves my original claim, which is the first sentence of this chapter: Most people are crazy. There's not a psychiatrist alive who'd even attempt to challenge my findings.

I'M AS BAD AS ANYONE. These days, you can basically measure my mood by the distance I'll let someone tailgate me before I slam on the brakes. On manic Monday, a safe distance behind me is a hundred car lengths.

Vick R. says, "When you're dealing with an asshole, make sure he's not doing the same thing." I need to work on that because when there's an asshole behind me, I guarantee there's a bigger asshole in front of him.

A word of caution though. Don't start something with a tailgater unless you're prepared to make a day of it. Remember, he's behind you, which means he gets to decide when it's over.

If he follows you to your destination, you may have to get out and fight. If you can't fight, you'll need to drive to the nearest police station and say you're being followed and everyone is out to get you. Sounds crazy to me.

WHEN ME AND VICK R. go to a meeting together, I insist on driving because I always need to be in control, which is a character defect I'm doing nothing to fix.

The need to be in control isn't a good trait to have, whether you're drinking or not. It's certainly not an attractive quality, and for Lisa's sake, I'm committed to working on it — but not until I'm damn good and ready.

As I was walking into the house one day, I decided it was time to clean out the garage. I went inside to set my stuff down. As I was going back out to get the leaf blower, Lisa came home and threw out a question that wasn't really a question.

"Honey, the garage is disgusting. Can you blow it out?"

Suddenly I didn't want to do it anymore, even though I was hellbent on doing it ten seconds earlier.

"I'm right in the middle of something," I said. "I'll do it tomorrow."

I DON'T KNOW why I feel in control when I'm driving. Control is the last thing I have when my hands are on the wheel. It wasn't always this way. It started the day I walked out of rehab without certain things I walked in there with – clear vision, short-term memory, depth perception and the motivation to get where I was going so I could drink.

For some reason, when I got sober, I forgot how to drive. Four years later, I still feel like a crash dummy behind the wheel sometimes. In fact, I brought a Kia Soul, so I wouldn't hurt anyone if I plowed into them.

When I first saw the little white thing sitting on the dealer's lot, I wanted to pick it up, bring it to the cash register and pay for it like a quart of milk.

The salesman saw me hovering over the "vehicle," and he walked up and asked me if I had any questions.

"Does it cost as much as a real car?"

He wanted to tell me about the gas mileage, the computer system and the resale value. I just wanted to talk about the airbags.

Seriously, it was my first question.

"It has airbags," he said. "Other than that, what did you want to know?"

"How many airbags does it have?"

"Two... one on the driver's side and one on the passenger side. That's the standard number of..."

"If this little thing hits a tree, I want airbags coming at me from every direction. I want to be bobbling around in there like an eight-year-old in a bouncy house."

It wouldn't be my first time in a rubber room.

I'm surprised Vick R. can even ride in my car without getting drunk first. At night, I have no idea where I am, who I am, where I'm going, what's in front of me or who the President is.

After marinating in alcohol for twenty-five years, the compass in my brain is rusted. The needle spins like a fan.

Vick R., on the other hand, is a human atlas. Name a place in Washington, Warren or Saratoga counties and he'll give you forty-seven different ways to get there. Once you choose one of the forty-seven routes, he'll still tell you about the other forty-six routes you could have taken.

One night, I picked him up for a meeting we'd gone to the week before, and the week before that. I didn't want him to know I forgot how to get there already.

On the way to his house, I programmed our destination into the GPS, with the volume off, so I could glance at it without him noticing. I figured he'd never catch on since he's almost seventy and still uses a flip phone.

Two minutes after picking him up, I came to an intersection and peeked at the GPS. It was telling me to turn right. Before I even hit the turn signal, he said, "No, don't turn right. It's taking you the wrong way. Go left."

Not once has Vick R. said, "Jesus Christ, how can you possibly be lost? We're in my driveway!"

He gets it. He understands what alcohol did to me. He knows that some things just don't come back -- like bearings, maturity, tact, erections, money... my wife could finish the list. Thankfully, she gets it too.

Vick R. should get a Purple Heart for staying composed when I drove him and Brian to Schuylerville in a snowstorm. From the air, my little white Kia must have looked like a jackrabbit running away from a bobcat in the snow, darting around and changing direction in midair.

It was pitch black, which didn't really matter. I was using the GPS like a video game, staring at the screen, trying to keep the little cartoon car on the purple line until I got to the checkered flag at the end. By the time we got there, Brian and Vick R. looked like they needed a drink.

It could have been worse. George could have been in the car. He's another one with an obsession with an atlas fetish. In fact, I've stopped telling George stories that involved places because he steals the flow of the stories by demanding the exact coordinates of everything. He's a story-killer.

It always goes something like this:

ME: *So, check this out. I was driving past the hardware store on Elm Street when a Sherman tank pulled into the intersection and turned its gun right at my windshield...*

GEORGE: *Is that the corner of Elm and Main Street or down by the Hess station?*

ME: *It's before the Hess station. Anyway, the tank fired a shot right over me and it obliterated the wall of the zoo and then a*

herd of elephants ran into the street and started playing
hopscotch on the sidewalk.

GEORGE: *The sidewalk by the park or on the river side?*

Taking another person's inventory, which is what I was just doing
to George, is exactly what the program of AA teaches us not to
do. But then, they don't encourage writing books about other
people in the program either -- unless the author gets their
permission.

I kinda did that. I suppose it's more accurate to say I got
permission to *mention* them in the book. I didn't tell them what I
was going to say. It doesn't matter. I changed (some of) their
names. Besides, they're all friends – the best kind of friends --
friends with no legal standing.

I took my own inventory in the last book and no one complained
that it was unfair to me. That book was about my character
defects. So is this one, but it's also about everyone else's. I've
found that the latter is both easier and more rewarding.

I let a couple people in this book choose their pseudonym –
including one rare bird who wanted to be called Aisling. Is that
anybody's real name?

They say that AA is a simple program for complicated people.
Intellectual achievement, they say, is often a hindrance to
"getting" the simple principles of the program – and brilliant
people often struggle with the program when they first walk into
the rooms.

Aisling is quick to remind everyone that she is one of those
brilliant people.

I'm not criticizing her. I do it too. In fact, I do it better than her. Hell, I wrote an entire book about my shortcomings, degrading myself with every sentence, then artfully weaved my accomplishments in between the degradations.

Look at all the dumb things this brilliant man did.

Aisling is a novice self-promoter, mostly because she tries to incorporate Long Island comedy and hipster phrases into her performances. In the Glans Falls area, that plays like a downstate act for an upstate schtick.

When she tries to be funny, she is – but only to herself and her smitten sponsees. A few months from now, I guarantee she'll say the same thing about me and this book.

Still, Aisling is one of the few people in the program who can make me laugh hard enough to be sore the next morning. She's smart enough to know the art of bad timing. Her best lines are delivered via whisper, right in the middle of a meeting, usually at a point where it would be most inappropriate to laugh.

I'm convinced she does it on purpose... that she waits for a quiet, emotional moment to lean over and drop a snide remark in my ear.

Maybe someone is talking about holding their hamster's paw as he took his final breath. That's when Aisling makes her move.

It's impossible to tune her out when her words are being direct-deposited from her mouth into my ear. Once she does that, I have to put my head down and gouge out my eyes to keep myself from laughing while the speaker is crying.

One time, she was telling me about a guy in the program who punched his probation officer.

"I believe that is a violation," I said.

"You're a lawyer?"

Snot came out of my nose. Pure brilliance. Prompt, obnoxious and flawless delivery. Those three things will make me explode every time.

George and Aisling would make a cute couple -- not *cute* cute, by any civilized standard, but certainly cute in the way they'd interact with each other in public, as a couple.

Any private interaction between them is just... I don't know, icky.

In my Neanderthal world, where hugs and drama and oversentimentality are anathema, it's the people I mock who mean the most to me.

It's warped, I know. I'm a work in progress. Dr. Stiller's potions *work*, but they don't work *miracles*.

I've laughed a lot in my four years of going to AA meetings, but only once did I start laughing at the beginning of a meeting and continue laughing at the same joke till the end of the meeting.

The perpetrator was one of my favorite people in the program, an old-timer named Wayne.

It was all in the delivery, a perfect example of "you had to be there."

We were reading the Twelve Steps at the beginning of the meeting, where one member reads a step, then passes it to the next member who reads the next step, and so on.

I read Step Three, passed it to Brian, who read Step Four, and he passed it to Wayne, who read Step Five. Wayne paused for a moment then handed it to George and softly whispered, "seven."

George looked at the paper with a dumbfounded, thousand-yard stare I'd kill to see again. At first, it was Wayne's gentle, helpful voice that got me. Then it was George's reaction. With one word, Wayne left George frozen stupid. For years I've been trying to get a reaction like that out of someone.

I knew I was in the right place – a place where an otherwise sophisticated seventy-year-old man can still act like a second-grader. It means I can stay there for another twenty years without changing a thing.

Chapter Eighteen

If You Build it, They Are Dumb

STILL FOUR YEARS SOBER

O ur South Glens Falls property isn't ideal for writing. It's only thirty-five miles from the lake house, but the two properties have as much in common as Hollywood and Appalachia, which isn't to suggest that one is better than the other. Frankly, I'd rather live in Appalachia.

Suburbia is an acquired taste and, several years after leaving the lake house, I was still struggling to acquire it. Everything was so clean and orderly and... lawful.

Apparently, my days of walking around the woods with a fig leaf and a rifle were over – but I figured, now that I was sober, I wouldn't want to do that stuff anyway. I was wrong.

Green lawns with trimmed hedges and paved driveways with Big Wheels are fine, I guess, but I prefer tall pines, dirt roads and ATVs. I need a forest, a place where I can yell unacceptable or unnatural things in a hundred different languages without suffering the consequences. I need a place where nothing is weird.

Looking at it from above, using Google Earth, our corner of South Glens Falls looks meticulous and deliberate, like some guy with a fully-loaded pocket protector laid the whole thing out on grid paper with a compass and a big metal ruler.

Three sides of our house are surrounded by wooded areas that give our neighbors a safe buffer from things like… me. It was those buffered areas that saved me from myself in the summer of 2016 and facilitated the writing of *You Can't Die: A Day of Clarity*.

That's when I sat down and started writing sober for the first time. It wasn't long before I got a visit from an ugly old friend: the dreaded mood spike.

Four years into sobriety, everything I hoped and expected to change did. The obsession to drink was gone; the shaking was gone; the stuttering was gone; and the daily interaction with police was gone. And, although the mood spikes never fully went away, they were minor, infrequent and easily manageable.

In the past, a mood spike could send me on a two-week spree of violence. It not only could, it did. But these days, with medication, the mood spikes were kinder and gentler. In fact, I'm pretty sure it was a mood spike that prompted my lemonade stand in the snow.

"Mood spike" is a term I coined, not because I'm a pioneer but because anything else makes it sound like I'm bipolar. It's something I've dealt with most of my adult life. It's nothing more than a sudden thought that causes a drastic mood change in me.

Why does any of that matter? Let's take a quick stroll down memory lane.

In 2003, I was sober for three months after going to rehab. It was my only period of sobriety before I stopped drinking permanently in 2013. I was at an AA meeting in an Albany church – laughing, having coffee and feeling great -- when I had a sudden mood change... a mood spike.

About fifteen minutes later, I had overdosed on Klonopin. My heart stopped beating in the church nave and later in the ambulance. It all happened quickly with no warning and, to this day, no real explanation from me.

The immediate result: I was mandated to a psychiatric facility and banned from my office in the State Capitol. I got a divorce and moved to my secluded lake house in the Adirondacks where I nearly drank myself to death.

The medications Dr. Stiller prescribed in 2014 have kept the mood spikes in check, but they weren't gone for good. I realized that in the while trying to write *You Can't Die: A Day of Clarity*.

After writing for about ten or fifteen minutes, a word must have triggered a thought and, suddenly, there was trouble on the flight deck.

It was as if some guy ran into the room, whispered "I'm gonna behead your mother," and ran away before I could kill him.

That's not the thought I had. I made it up because I don't remember what the thought really was. I just remember that it was that dark. That's a mood spike. It's the kind of thing that used to send me on some sort of dangerous rampage.

If I had any chance of writing an entire book, I had to find a way to ignore mood spikes and snap out of it quickly, without losing my train of thought.

At first, I tried shouting them away and slapping myself on the side of the head. I even yodeled a few times. That can be dangerous in a house where someone is always running around recording stuff.

Luckily, no one caught me managing my mood spikes that summer. It's not the way I wanted to go viral on YouTube or Reddit... again. More on that in a bit.

MOOD SPIKES MADE IT HARDER to write my first book but, in the summer of 2016, they gave rise to a great empire known as "The Ranch."

It all started one morning when a mood spike sent me running into the woods behind the house, where I started pushing down dead pine trees. Disclaimer: If you're going to do that, understand that the top of the tree can break off and fall on your head.

I barely dodged that bullet. It would have truly sucked if Lisa had to eulogize me by explaining how I wound up looking like a deli sandwich spiked with a toothpick.

The next day, I found a safer weapon to ward off dark thoughts: A hatchet. That's what I grabbed when a mood spike struck two minutes after I sat down.

I was out there for about ten minutes, hacking away at a tree that was big enough to withstand me, my mood spikes and my hatchet for an hour or two.

Once it felt like my thoughts were safely back in place – and having made a respectable dent in the tree -- I went back inside and started writing again.

It was about ninety degrees that day, and I had wood chips and dying mosquitos stuck to the sweat on my arms. The writer William Styron said, "Let's face it, writing is hell." Whatever, Willy. Try cutting down a tree in between paragraphs.

I had to run back out to the woods another five times that day, and it only yielded two pages, but they were good pages, and, at the end of the day, I had the honor of yelling "timber" as the tree crashed to the ground.

It's not an efficient way to write, and it's not great for the environment, but it was working for me.

Still, solutions are supposed to solve problems, whereas my solutions were creating more of them. I couldn't cut down trees forever without turning our property into a pasture – and clear-cutting someone *else's* property seems rude.

That was Problem One. Problem Two was figuring out what to do with the trees I'd already cut down. Before solving that problem, I decided to create another one. To speed up the process of killing time by killing trees, I put down the hatchet and replaced it with a Sawzall.

In less than a day, I had *twice* as much lumber – and I still hadn't come up with an idea about what to do with it.

That's the problem with me. My solutions do the opposite of what solutions are supposed to do: they make things worse.

It's like filling your house with bats to get rid of the mosquitos. It'll work, but now you'll need a bunch of racoons to get rid of the bats. After that, you'll need cougars to kill the racoons. To get rid of the cougars, you'll need hunters.

What are you left with? A house full of rednecks with shotguns. And you still have mosquitos because the racoons ate all the bats.

Hence, I had a Sawzall to create more unwanted lumber.

In 1982, I went to a Police concert. The opening band, the Fixx, started the show off with their hit single, "One Thing Leads to Another." I should make that the Ranch's provisional anthem, because it's the premise upon which it was built.

A Sawzall, of course, is the precursor to a chainsaw and a backhoe. I don't have either of those but, as Cicero taught, *Nec rutrum usus currus circumdatos.* "When you don't have a backhoe, use a riding mower."

At least, I *think* it was Cicero of Rome. Maybe it was Grady of Chestertown.

A week later, I was on the mower, plowing through the woods with the blades running, sending gusts of shredded leaves and chipped wood flying in every direction.

I had an ax in one hand and a pruner in the other. The Sawzall, impersonating a chainsaw, was on hand just in case I decided to bring down one of the bigger trees that appeared to be in my way.

It sounds like I was out of control, and I was. But I wasn't carelessly clearcutting. The wooded area I was cutting in was overgrown with trees competing for sunlight. The "green" in me felt compelled to point that out.

Once I created a large open area, I decided to use all the lumber to build a ranch – like a dude ranch, but without the "dude" because it sounds so pussy-ish.

Every day, I'd write for a half hour, then run outside for a half hour of "ranching," turning trees into logs, logs into posts, posts into fences and fences into "The Ranch."

It must have been a curious sight to people passing by... me turning the wooded buffer zones between the houses in a quiet neighborhood into a federal project on the Appalachian Trail.

With all this going on, one thing was unquestionably happening around the dining room tables of our neighbors. I could see mom or dad opening the dinner hour with a roundtable discussion on the matter.

MOM: *Okay, let's go around the table and share our theories about what the big sweaty man with the tattoos is doing. We'll start with you, Billy.*

BILLY: *I don't know, mom, but I'm wetting my bed again. Can I go live with Grandma and Grandpa?*

MOM: *Yes, you can, but only until we have him arrested for something. How about you, honey?*

DAD: *I called the Town Zoning Office. They said they've already turned the matter over to the police, and the police said they turned it over to the Department of Mental Health.*

MOM: *Did you call the Department of Mental Health?*

DAD: *Yeah, they said they're looking for someone <u>they</u> can turn it over to.*

BY THE END OF the following summer, the spot where I ran into the woods and pushed down my first dead tree was one of three grand entranceways to "The Ranch," a rodeo-sized retreat behind the house that saved me from a life of watering marigolds and waving to the paperboy.

Each entranceway consists of ten-foot-tall posts whose tops are bridged with a fifteen-foot maple arc. The central entrance is marked with a four-foot Ranch sign. It leads to the main part of the Ranch, which is the size of a large helipad.

I transplanted a dozen ferns to the center of the ranch for a raised garden with its own little fence.

Since the Ranch sits on what used to be hundreds of acres of strawberry patches, there are no stones, so I had to import bowling ball-size boulders from the lake house for the obligatory firepit.

There are a lot of other things in the ranch -- benches, tables, games – all made from trees, rail spikes, deck screws and spar – a lot of spar.

There's even a stage – a real one. It's not just some platform you can stand on; it's a ten-foot, multi-tiered log stage, with a side stairway and a fan-design marquee. It's strong enough to hold a car... well, *my* car. It doesn't need to be; it just is.

The ranch even has a ceiling, of sorts. The design is like a circus tent, with a twenty-foot king post in the center of the ranch circle. It serves as the junction for a network of long bannisters and thick vines connected to trees on the perimeter of the ranch fence.

Everything I've just described is the "The Ranch" – or, what I call, "the head of the tadpole."

Why tadpole? From the air, that's what the full Ranch compound looks like... a three-hundred-foot tadpole.

The tail of the tadpole is the "Ranch Trail," which begins at a three-foot opening on one side of the ranch and turns into a winding, fenced-in trail that runs through the woods surrounding our property.

The trail is about the length of a football field and fifteen feet wide in some parts. The fence is double-railed in most places and triple-railed in others. The posts are pine and the rails are mostly maple and birch.

A thirty-foot section of the trail is made with a rabbit fence design, comprised of long thin branches. It has movable gates at both ends and I use it as dog pen for Bam and Molly every so often, just to keep them at one with nature.

The Ranch Trail even has an "Owl's Nest" viewing station. The owl that lived there is humongous. If Molly ever disappears, I know where to look for her... or not to.

Right near the entrance to the Ranch, there's a Ranch Office. It used to be a shed, but I emptied it, painted the floors, walls and ceiling, then added heat, electric, lights, stereo, chairs and carpets.

In the year I spent building the Ranch, I shrugged off the same questions a thousand times.

What the fuck are you doing?

I'll tell you when I'm done.

What's it for?

What it for? I hate that question. There's a guy named Oscar in the rooms. He's in his eighties and he likes to paint. I've seen several of his little canvas paintings. I'm no connoisseur, but he's pretty damn good.

I'm not sure where he gets his inspiration, but I think it comes from what he hears in the rooms. At least twice, I've seen him give his paintings as gifts to people who were struggling.

The last time Oscar brought in a painting, one of AA's resident busybodies started badgering the shit out of him.

"Oh, these are very good. You could get a booth permit at the arts festival in Lake George. Have you thought about joining a coop? You should also be posting these online and emailing them to freelance forums. Do you have a scanner? You can get a good high definition..."

"Oh my God, shut the fuck up lady!" That's what I was about to say when, thank God, the gavel banged to start the meeting.

Poor Oscar looked so overwhelmed and uncomfortable. Why can't Oscar just paint a farm scene for a friend in the program because he wants to? Isn't that good enough?

I'm not comparing myself to Oscar. He's a sweet man. His intentions are sincerer than mine will ever be.

What we have in common is a willingness to invest without a return. Not everything is *for* something. Maybe it's just for fun. Not everything requires a feasibility study. Maybe you should just do it and see what happens.

Half of the great things in this world happened by accident, including Jackson.

The Ranch didn't make sense to a lot of people while I was building it. On paper, it still doesn't. I can't imagine how a realtor would deal with it.

Beautiful four-bedroom home, three baths and open kitchen with spacious deck and large front yard... all of which backs up to a rustic, sort of western-style... area with scenic trail that... with a stage for perfect for... MUST SEE!

Something doesn't need a reason to have a purpose. The Ranch is a byproduct of my writing, and my writing is a byproduct of the ranch. I needed one to do the other. What I don't need is approval.

It's like doodling on a piece of paper while sitting in class at Harvard Law School. One day, maybe you'll be a rich lawyer, but maybe people will like your art more than your reputation in the courtroom.

The mood spikes that interrupted the writing of my first book produced two tangible rewards: the book itself, which I wrote while dripping with sweat; and the coolest back yard in the neighborhood.

WHEN THE GROUND FROZE in early Fall, I winterized the Ranch in plastic, moved the entire operation inside and began carving wood in the basement.

By then, I'd already completed the first book, and I was contemplating this one.

I don't know what it is about wood, but I knew I wouldn't be able to write a word unless there was something to redirect the mood spikes. I needed something to carve or cut down in between paragraphs and chapters. It had become a habit. With me, everything is a habit, but this one didn't come in cans and bottles.

My carvings weren't very creative. I was limited by my skills, of course. The first thing I carved was an AA gavel for George's one-year anniversary of being sober.

George asked me to chair that celebration, but I was a little late getting there because the polyurethane on the gavel was still wet. I had it sitting in a paper bag at the head table with me and George.

Someone in the front row said she smelled gas. It was just the polyurethane, but I wasn't going to ruin the surprise. Of course, if the gavel stuck to George's hand when I gave it to him, the cat and the gavel would be out of the bag.

I spoke first, then George spoke, and I presented him with his one-year coin. You're supposed to hug people at that point in the program, and I didn't want to defy protocol in front of so many people.

I tried to give him a guy hug with a couple of pats on the back. He wanted more. He pulled me in for a full-blown embrace. Then, for the sole purpose of being an ass, he kissed me -- not directly on the lips, but close to the lips... and I felt his tongue touch the corner of my mouth.

Everyone got a rise out of that – not literally, I hope – and there was a lot of laughing and I just wanted to throw up.

I presented George with his damp gavel. That's when it got quiet and awkward in the room. I used that quiet time to wonder why in the fuck I was presenting George with a gavel. It symbolizes absolutely nothing.

Everyone was just staring at me. I guess they were waiting for me to explain the significance.

"It's because I didn't feel like buying a card," I told them. "Eat your cake."

FIRST IT WAS GEORGE'S GAVEL, then an old-style Billy club and then a penis. I'm talking about my carvings. Why a penis? Don't judge. I was going to carve my face, but I couldn't carve and look at my face at the same time.

I didn't want to carve someone's else's face, and I definitely didn't want to carve someone else's penis. It's was a no-brainer. I just had to be ~~circumspect~~ careful with the knife.

Today, I have about forty gavels, ten Billy clubs, four walking sticks, one guitar body... and the penis.

I've seen a lot of crappy, boring gavels in the rooms of AA. My plan was to donate every one of my beautifully-carved, stained

253

and polyurethaned oak gavels to the groups. By the time this book came out, I hadn't donated a single gavel to anyone, even though I was swimming in them.

Mark Hoyt, my first wrestling coach and mentor, used to say, "You're only as good as what you leave behind."

I can hear Jackson and Mallory after I die, when they see what I left behind.

MALLORY: *What the hell are we going to do with all these damn gavels?*

JACKSON: *If he wanted to be useful, he should have used all this wood to make his own casket.*

Chapter Nineteen

Boon's Day in the Day

MORE THAN FOUR YEARS SOBER

C hick... is that you Chick?"

That was the prelude to a conversation between a biker and a wrestling coach that can best be described as... well, memorable.

If I live for a thousand years, I'll never forget a word of it.

It happened at George's first Alcoholics Anonymous meeting. (A lot of people knew George as "Chick," including Boon.)

Ever since Boon eased my mind about Jackson a couple years earlier, I was always glad to see him coming through the door. Boon was a staple in the rooms of AA. He looked like a cross between President Taft and a Hell's Angel. He was perpetually poised and had a reassuring presence.

George is a humble guy. He hated it when I referred to him as "a Hudson Falls legend," so when Boon walked up, I introduced him as "Hudson Falls' legendary wrestling coach."

That seemed to catch Boon's attention.

"Back in the day, I worked at a bar called the Garrison with a guy named George. He coached wrestling around here. You probably know him. George Chikanis was his name."

"Back in the day" was Boon's trademark expression. Everything he said either began or ended with it.

Turns out, back in the 70s, when George and Boon were around twenty years old, Boon was a bartender at a Lake George bar and George was his bouncer.

Boon didn't make the connection right away.

"He was a big Greek guy," Boon said, "and we called him Chick."

"Yeah, that was me," said George.

"He worked the front door, back in the day," said Boon.

"*I'm* Chick," said George.

"Yeah, we called him Chick, and he always had my back, that George Chikanis."

Finally, I decided to break up the Abbott and Costello routine.

I grabbed George by the back of the neck and looked Boon straight in the eye.

"This is George Chikanis! This is Chick!"

Boon's face lit up. He stepped back, staring in amazement at George, like he was Jesus.

"Chick?"

"You're looking at him," said George.

Boon, the king of cool and composure, was overcome with emotion. He was giddy.

"Chick… is that you Chick?"

George was smiling ear to ear. Boon's eyes were wide open and glistening.

"Yes, Boon, it's me. I remember you well."

I'd never seen Boon so happy. It was as if William Harley and Arthur Davidson walked in the door with a giftwrapped set of new pipes.

And, even in the misery of early sobriety, George seemed just as happy.

I tried to imagine Boon sliding beer bottles down the bar, while big George worked the door and broke up fights. That was forty years ago, when I was ten.

I was already seated next to George when the meeting started. Boon grabbed the chair next to me, so he could keep talking to "Chick."

Now I was seated between the reunited lovebirds, passing messages back and forth every time one of them didn't hear the other. I felt like a third wheel.

Several months after that, Boon was driving his Harley back to Queensbury from the Daytona 500 in Florida. He was almost home – about an hour away – when a young driver pulled out in front of him at an intersection.

It was a tough pill for a lot of people in the rooms to swallow, including the author. One of Boon's great gifts was empathy. He was an intent listener. Whenever I spoke to Boon, his eyes and his attention were aimed squarely at me and what I was saying.

Back in the day, Boon had escaped death countless times. Doctors always pieced him together, so he could run back to the garage and tend to his mangled Harley.

Boon didn't talk too much about God or his Higher Power. He talked about his bikes, his sobriety and the program that saved his life.

I truly believe that some Higher Power put George in Boon's path before he was killed. They both needed it, but Boon needed it more.

Boon didn't want to go backwards. He didn't want to glorify his drinking. He just wanted a glimpse of a past that – even with all its wreckage -- still had fond memories.

George and Boon had a lot of fun in those days. Boon used to say that all the time and he wasn't ashamed of it. He wanted to believe that his reminiscing wasn't misplaced, that his yesterdays weren't wasted. George provided the proof when he showed up at Boon's doorstep that day and confirmed everything Boon said about how it was, back in the day.

Chapter Twenty

A Funny Thing Happened on the Way Back to Detox

FOUR YEARS AND TWO MONTHS SOBER

One of the few things I remember from my days at Springfield College was an English class that my professor called "Varsity Rhetoric."

He once told us that "only two percent of the population could use a simple word like paradox in a sentence, and only one percent will ever need to." For thirty years, I proved him right, until I got this pair of texts from Courtney one Saturday night.

"I don't want to drink anymore."

"Where are you," I asked.

"Bruno's."

Bruno's is a bar, of course. Hence, the paradox.

I don't even remember how I met Courtney. She was in AA for a long time, then she was in jail for a short time, then she was back in AA, and then she was back in jail.

The day before Courtney's paradoxical text, she messaged me from her apartment, which, coincidentally, is right above Juan's.

"I think I need to go to the hospital detox. Can you bring me, or should I ask Juan?"

"I'm coming home from the lake," I told her. "Can you hang on for an hour?"

"Yeah, I'm just lying in bed drinking."

She was the only one lying. I wasn't coming home from the lake. I was digging a post hole on the ranch.

Juan sent me a text five minutes earlier, saying there was a problem at the house, and I didn't want to commit to anything until I found out what was going on.

Finally, after not hearing back from Juan, I told her I was on my way. I knew she'd be drunk when I got there, which was fine. Most detoxes won't even take you unless you're completely bombed.

She called me when I was halfway there.

"I'm gonna bring booze with me because it's my last hurrah and I don't want to go through withdrawal until they have me hooked up to IVs."

Yeah, it was my last hurrah a thousand times too. Only an alcoholic would consider it a "hurrah" to drink alone in a hospital linen closet.

Paradox Courtney was hoping to get weaned off alcohol with Ativan, the same narcotic they used on me. I was pretty sure Glens Falls Hospital wouldn't do that, but I was hoping they could get her into an Albany detox when they got a glimpse of her withdrawal symptoms.

I was two minutes away when she texted me again.

"I'm in trouble. Please hurry. I'm not okay."

Oh, okay Courtney... in that case, I'll hurry instead of pulling every fifty feet and counting backward from one hundred.

I pulled on to Paradox Courtney and Juan's street.

I didn't expect to see police cars in front of the house. Now I knew what she meant by "trouble" and why she wanted me to hurry.

My first thought was that she did something to herself, but when I got closer, I saw Juan talking to a group of officers by the door.

As soon as Juan saw my car, he pointed at me and the cops glared at me like everything was my fault. Turned out, they just wanted me to take her to the hospital, thereby making Courtney my problem instead of theirs. Meanwhile, I was looking for a way to make Courtney Juan's problem instead of mine.

Once I got out of my car, the cops got into theirs and left. It's the first time the police were ever happy to see me.

"What's with the police?" I asked Juan.

"My woman called Five-0. Courtney threated her."

"There's a surprise... your woman calling the police. What's her problem?"

"No, no, she said Courtney threatened..."

I interrupted him because I knew it was the other way around.

"Whatever!"

I was pissed at him for letting his "woman" call the police on Courtney for the thousandth time.

It's hard with Juan, though. Whenever I try to argue with him, he just agrees with everything I say.

I'll say, "You need to get your own apartment."

He'll say, "I know, damn!"

Then I'll say, "Then do it."

And he'd say, "That's what I'm gonna do."

How the fuck can you argue with that?

I went upstairs, and Paradox Courtney was looking around her apartment the way a dog looks for the tennis ball you pretended to throw.

"I'm almost ready," she said, fumbling with her cell phone and a knapsack.

"My mom is on the phone and she's been reading your book. She wants to talk to you."

I was positive there was no one on the other end of the phone. I grabbed it from her so she'd use both hands to get ready.

A voice was yelling "Courtney! Courtney!"

"Hello ...uh, Courtney's mom?"

She started to talk but I wasn't really listening because I was concentrating on getting Paradox Courtney's attention, so she could see the nasty look I was giving her.

She saw it and laughed. She was way too drunk to give a shit.

"You don't sound like the person who wrote this book," her mom said.

"I haven't said anything yet."

"Well, thank you for taking care of her. She needs your kind of help."

"She needs better help than that," I said, waiting for a laugh and not getting one.

There's never a good time to do difficult things. If you're an alcoholic, there's nothing harder than getting sober and staying sober. It's harder for some than it is for others, and for Courtney, it was going to be extremely hard, just as it was for me.

"Can we stop for beer?"

"I thought you had vodka in your knapsack," I said.

"Well, yeah, but..."

I get it. It's like having butter without the bread.

I pulled into Cumberland Farms. If I had refused, I guarantee she would have changed her mind about detox and jumped out of the car. Four years ago, that's what I would have done.

As soon as an alcoholic feels the booze leaving their system, any thoughts about getting sober fly right out the window.

"Listen," I told her, "I'm not going in there to buy it for you, and I don't think anyone in there is dumb enough to sell you alcohol right now."

She rolled her eyes, pushed back her hair and grabbed her wallet.

"Watch this."

I gotta hand it to her. She walked through the door like she was the branch manager checking on her employees. Two minutes later, she walked out with her beer.

"Don't open a beer in the car," I told her.

"You're going the wrong way."

I pulled over to program my GPS.

"You're kidding me," she said. "Just go straight, veer to the right and we're there."

"Shut up. You're the one who's drunk."

"You'd never know it by the way you're driving."

As we turned into the hospital, I tried to give her a little advice.

"Don't go in there asking for Ativan. Just exaggerate your withdrawal symptoms and they'll prob…"

"Where the are you going now?" she yelled, as I barreled past the obvious emergency room entrance.

You would think that, given all the times I'd been on helicopters with the Governor, I would know that round parking lots… aren't parking lots.

"I know what I'm doing." I said.

People were staring at us. I was driving around on the Mercy Flight helipad.

"You want to fly, is that it?" she said, laughing at her own joke.

I needed to turn around. I did a U-Turn that was more of a W-Turn followed by a E-Turn. Since we were on a helipad, I could have just done an O-Turn.

After a few more awkward maneuvers, I got Paradox Courtney into the emergency room. I didn't hear from her again until seven o'clock that evening.

For a lot of hardcore alcoholics, the ER is often the first step on the path to recovery. Ideally, Courtney's sequence of treatment should have gone something like this: emergency room, detox, rehab, halfway house, Alcoholics Anonymous.

JP Bruno's Bar is nowhere on that list, but that's where Paradox Courtney called me from five hours later.

She sounded just like I must have sounded a hundred times, after running away from hospitals, detoxes and rehabs. She was changing the subject from drinking to some other problem, acting as if our trip to the ER never happened.

"I'm just hanging out here for a while," she said. "I need your advice something."

"Okay."

"I'm trying to get my boyfriend to stop smoking."

I used to do the same thing. I could play that game too.

"Yeah, it's gonna kill him," I said. "Has he thought of Chantix?"

"It's not just the smoking. We've been going through…"

"Wait, before I forget. How did things go in the emergency room?"

"Oh yeah. It was okay. No Ativan there. They kept me for a few hours and said I should go to St. Peter's. I'm gonna Uber my way there tonight."

Yeah, right. Do we even have Uber in Glens Falls?

"I wouldn't do that. It's an hour away. And, trust me, they won't admit you unless you're hammered."

"Oh, I know," she said. "I'll let you know when I'm settled in over there."

I texted her an hour later, but didn't hear back until the next day, when she sent me a bunch of upbeat texts from St. Peter's Hospital – the kind of texts you might expect from someone who got her Ativan.

That's twice I had to hand it to her. I didn't think it was a good idea in the middle of the night. I have no idea how she got there, but now she was in a hospital that was equipped to deal with her.

"I feel great. I don't want to drink. I'm going to do this."

Reading her texts was agitating me because I knew exactly what she was going through. I also knew her texts would stop coming in a few days when they stopped giving her Ativan.

That's when the hell begins. I hoped it would end sooner for her than it did for me.

PARADOX COURTNEY looks like a Kindergarten teacher. It's hard to picture her in an orange jumpsuit. But she's a chronic alcoholic and, even though her original offense didn't warrant jail time, her probation violations did. What were her probation violations? Testing positive for alcohol. Run that through your brain a few times. Could we at least have a system that looks like someone designed it on purpose?

Every time Paradox Courtney got sent to jail, it was for drinking. Her original crime was "drinking-related," but it didn't warrant jail time, just probation. Drinking is a probation violation. She couldn't quit, so they kept sending her to jail.

DWI is a serious offense, but the penalty for driving after two glasses of wine shouldn't be the same as beating someone with a hammer. The drug problem is equally serious, but you don't solve it by incarcerating the people who are addicted.

It's a political problem and, having worked in the Governor's Office for a decade, I know a thing or two about those.

From the Second-Floor office of the State Capitol, those of us in the Governor's Office had a good view of the many protests on the plaza. We usually mocked the protesters and we had a damn good reason to – it was fun.

But, I never mocked the protesters calling for the repeal the Rockefeller Drug Laws, which mandated ridiculously long prison sentences for drug possession. As loud as they were, I never criticized them because they were right. The Governor agreed with them too, privately.

I know quite a few people who have overdosed on heroin and died. It's tough for addicts and alcoholics to get help when they're competing with a state that's hellbent on putting them in prison.

Everyone supports "protecting children from drugs," until *their* children have a problem and need protection from the criminal justice system.

That's when they realize the system is more dysfunctional than the disease.

Chapter Twenty-One

OMG, Did You Hear What Joe Said About Frank???

STILL FOUR YEARS AND TWO MONTHS SOBER

Drama is everywhere, including the rooms of Alcoholic Anonymous. When your network of friends consists of a hundred or so addicts and alcoholics, there's going to be an occasional conflict. Rarely are they anything of substance, unless it's substance abuse. It's like anywhere else... *he said this, she said that, he's having sex with blah blah blah.*

Aside from the sex thing, who cares?

"Let me ask you something," George said as we were heading to Saratoga.

"Okay, I'm letting you."

He cleared his throat, so I knew it wasn't going to be brief and it would just be a matter of time before I'd want to drive into a bridge.

"You sure? It's personal."

"I'm driving; I can't give you a drumroll."

"Are you mad at Brian?"

Sigh.

As gym teachers and coaches, Brian and George spent their entire careers in high schools and now it was starting to show. Schools are like prisons, where the guards become like the inmates, and now I was getting the kind of question you'd hear Becky asking Britney in the lunchroom.

I was cringing. Am I mad at Brian? I wasn't, but I also wasn't about to lengthen this conversation by giving him an answer. At the same time, I didn't want to be insensitive or rude. I chose my words carefully.

"Get the fuck out of my car."

I don't have a problem with sensitive or personal discussions. I just can't have them about personality conflicts, especially when there isn't one. It's a bad hobby. My abhorrence for it isn't a *guy* thing; it's a *me* thing, and it's not just a me thing. Charles is the same way.

One time me and Charles were on our way to New York City. He was driving, and I was just doing... whatever. After forty-five minutes of nice, relaxing silence, Charles had something to say, so he said it.

"The best part of being a guy is we can go an hour without talking, and neither one of us is going to say, *'Did I do something wrong?'*"

That's why Charles and I never fight.

MY FRIENDS AND ACQUAINTANCES in AA and NA range in age from eighteen to eighty-five. I've heard all their stories and I've identified with some more than others.

I've seen young people who remind me of how I was, middle-age people that remind me of who I am and older people who conjure visions of who I'll be.

You'd think I'd predict being like my sponsor one day. I wouldn't have picked a sponsor who makes me think of myself in twenty years. I needed someone to help me be less like me, not more like him.

If I wanted an older version of me, I'd have asked my father to sponsor me. That was never an option for a litany of reasons, not the least of which is that he's dead. I guess that would be the main reason.

I'll probably be a lot like Barry. If you want to know who Barry is, run into his church waving a pistol. Barry is the one shooting you in the teeth.

In the late 1970's, while I was reaching puberty, Barry came into the program with an attitude that was even worse than mine when I got there thirty years later. He was constantly saying, "Life sucks and then you die." I was constantly saying, "Death is funny." You won't hear Joel Osteen quoting either of us.

Barry was in the military and law enforcement, so he's crossed paths with his fair share of pricks. God only knows how he dealt with them – probably like I used to – but, over the years, he's developed an equanimity that I want – that I need -- to emulate.

When Wayne talks about rock bottom, he compares it to an elevator. Everyone is different, he says. "I went as far down as I was willing to go and got off somewhere in the middle."

Yeah, well, I never even pushed a button and crashed in the basement.

It's impossible to be both Jesus and Cesar, but if I shut up long enough, I might gain wisdom from roughness, knowledge from obstinance and maybe even tenderness from douchebaggery. If I can do all that, I just might be a ~~sane~~ responsible man someday.

The important words are "so far." The *responsible* train hasn't left the station yet. It's not even on the tracks. Now and in the foreseeable future, life is what life is – a victory lap with no finish line, a time to spread the good news and celebrate what I almost threw away.

Chapter Twenty-Two

A Bridge to Narcan

None of the medications I take are narcotics. As an alcoholic, those are off limits to me – forever. The conventional wisdom is that, if you're an addict or alcoholic, any mind-altering substance will lead you right back to your drug of choice.

It's common sense, right. If you're a recovering meth addict, you should not be getting drunk after NA meetings. If you're a recovering alcoholic, you're not really sober if you're smoking pot. You can't substitute one drug for another.

Here's where it gets dicey. What if you're an alcoholic and you need surgery? It's a no-brainer, right. You're going to need some sort of morphine because Tylenol isn't going to cut it.

It took me more than four years of sobriety to summon the courage to go to a dentist. It's something I'd been afraid to do ever since I took a stab at being my own dentist.

It happened on a Saturday night in the winter of 2012. I was drunk, of course, and I had a toothache – a bad molar. I couldn't get anyone to look at it.

I was at the lake house, and Lisa, Michael and Rachel were there. Since there wasn't anything they could do to help, I decided to yank the thing out myself.

Lisa and I had been together for less than a year. I hadn't corrupted her yet. She still lived in a world where everything was sensible and wholesome and safe.

She was still the mom who insisted on plastic covers on outlets, parental blocks on TVs and warm toasty mittens on chilly days. In her world, everything was in perfect order; everything was by the book, risk-free and government-approved.

So, when I walked in the living room with pliers saying I was going to "do an extraction," she was horrified.

"I can't watch this!"

"I just need you to hand me gauze while a manipulate the tooth."

It wasn't really gauze; it was crumpled up toilet paper.

The other instruments included a pair of pliers, a small chisel and a vascular clamp.

I stole the clamp from my father's old medical school bag when I was on break from college. My friends and I used it as a giant roach clip, so we could smoke joints right down to the last speck of weed.

I wasn't performing heart surgery, so I didn't really need the clamp, but it was the only thing I could properly sterilize. Plus, I wanted Lisa to think I knew what I was doing, and it made my instrument tray (a frying pan) look professional.

The procedure took about twenty minutes. I didn't realize how hard it was going to be. It wasn't the pain that made it difficult; it was the was the amount of muscle I had to put into it.

The worst part was the chisel. I had to use it like a pry bar against my healthy tooth. It produced a hard-to-ignore grinding sound, which made it seem like the healthy tooth was going to snap before the bad one did.

Then there was the cracking noise when the bad tooth finally snapped. I thought I pulled out a piece of my jaw.

I'm not sure why I was surprised. When you jam a chisel between your teeth, you should expect complications.

Every dentist I've seen since Chisel Day has looked in my mouth and said something along the lines of, "What happened in here? It looks like there was a terror attack on your mouth."

Chisel Day, will have the redeeming value of being funny. I finally went to the dentist in 2018. The tooth I pulled was perfectly healthy. She showed it to me on the x-rays.

"The root is still there and it's fine," she said. "You probably had a piece of food stuck in there somewhere."

Lmao.

"Good thing I got a second opinion this time. I was getting ready to pull this one too."

As she was nosing around in my mouth, she hit me with a trick question.

"When did you have the bridge put in?"

"I have a bridge? What's a bridge?"

She explained what it was. Apparently, when I was dentist-hopping in 2012, one of them kept me in the chair long enough to construct a bridge over the tooth I pulled.

I always wondered what happened to the gap in the back of my mouth. I figured it grew back because I didn't get enough of the root. Seriously, that's what I thought.

Apparently, the dentist who built my bridge in 2012 was as drunk as I was.

"He didn't put it in right. It's uneven," she said. "Your dental bridge is falling down."

She thought that was funny.

I wound up going to another dentist because the Tooth Comedian was too eager to start ripping shit out of my mouth.

The new dentist told me all about the nerve pathways in the mouth and the strange way the nerves delegate pain to random places around your face.

I won't try to explain what I don't understand, even though I did it in the Governor's Office for a decade. In a nutshell, the nerve that was causing the pain was nowhere near the pain itself. It's like getting stabbed in the right leg and feeling the pain in your left hand.

In other words, I ripped out a tooth because it hurt, but the pain was coming from… I don't know, Bam's mouth.

The dentist said first thing I needed was a root canal.

They scheduled it for a week later. To keep me reasonably sane in the interim, the dentist prescribed a narcotic pain medication called hydrocodone.

For some alcoholics – *some* -- taking a narcotic is no different than downing a shot of Jack Daniels. As soon as they get a few of them in their system, the addictive gene takes over, and when their prescription runs out, they either get them illegally or go back to drinking. It happens all the time. I've seen it.

So, in February of 2018, after four years and five months of being strict and vigilant in situations like this, I had to weigh the severity of my pain versus the risk of sabotaging my sobriety.

It was my biggest predicament since Mr. Haiku sprayed Saki down my throat four years earlier. It demanded better judgment than when I stepped toward the slot machines in Las Vegas – also four years earlier – where the cocktail waitresses were passing out free beer.

I won't say I dropped the ball, but I definitely bobbled it.

I convinced myself that the hydrocodone wouldn't be any more addictive than the nitrous oxide I'd be inhaling when they did the root canal. I filled the prescription.

It's a good idea to tell another alcoholic or addict when you're putting yourself at risk. If I was going on a five-day hike in the Adirondacks, I would tell someone exactly where I was headed, so they'd know where to look for me if I never came back.

In this case, I needed someone to look for me at the nearest bar if I never came back from filling my prescription. I told Suzie, one of my closest friends in the program. She'd been clean for two years after struggling with opioid addiction. Hydrocodone is an opioid.

While I'm patting myself on the back for making a good decision, I should admit that I leapfrogged three better decisions to get there.

1) I should have told the dentist I was an alcoholic; 2) In addition to telling Suzie, I should have called my sponsor. 3) I should have told Suzie *before* I took my first dose, not after.

"I'm taking hydrocodone," I told her. "There was no way around it."

There actually *was* a way around it. I could have just, umm, not taken it.

"Why, what happened?" she asked.

I told her about the pain and I may have exaggerated the severity of it. I wasn't really throwing up and bleeding from the eyes.

It's going to take a lot more than a few pain pills to make me drink again. For me, having just one pint of beer would be equivalent to drinking a pint of gasoline, then lighting a cigarette.

Still, I danced with the devil. At the very least, I cock-teased him a little. I can't make it a habit.

I'm still an alcoholic, complete with an alcoholic brain and alcoholic thinking. I told Suzie first because I thought she'd say it was no big deal. She didn't say that. She told me to flush the pills down the toilet.

So, I called someone else. Just like I always do, I went shopping for a better answer. I told Vick R. about the hydrocodone the next day. He said if the pain is unbearable, and I needed to take the meds, I should do it.

"We didn't quit drinking to suffer," he told me.

That's the answer I was looking for. Well, it was half the answer Ii was looking for. The pain wasn't *technically* unbearable, but I didn't listen to that part.

Had he given me the same answer as Suzie, I would have called Juan, then George and then some random number.

I don't drink like an alcoholic anymore, but I need to stop thinking like one. This is a tricky disease. It's in my best interest not to fuck with it.

Chapter Twenty-Three

My Viral Disease

FOUR YEARS AND THREE MONTHS SOBER

Back in 2016, news of my lemonade stand in the snow made its way into the rooms quickly. My sponsor learned about it on the evening news, which ran a picture, along with their own color commentary. He thought it was funny, but I think he also thought it was more than that. He jokingly said -- I *think* he was joking -- to "keep coming back," something old timers say to newcomers when their alcoholic behavior flares up.

The following winter, temperatures dropped to negative numbers in South Glens Falls, so I told Lisa it was time for a taco stand. That's not my old alcoholic behavior talking.

The heart wants what the heart wants, and my heart wanted a taco stand, even though I never eat tacos. In fact, the last time I had a taco was in 1996 at a Taco Bell just three miles from the Mexican border. I ate the taco in Chula Vista, California, and threw it up in Tijuana, Mexico. I think I did it backwards.

Half the fun is making the signs, and mine were big and brilliant in their basicness, using tempera paint sticks and crooked block print in colors from the Mexican flag.

I waited for it to warm up before setting up my stand at the end of the driveway. When it hit five degrees, I got undressed. I originally planned on wearing nothing but a bandana, shorts and flip flops, but the wind chill made it a lot colder than five degrees, so I threw on a tank top.

I couldn't find a sombrero anywhere, despite the white trash folklore that Walmart has "ever-thin." The closest thing to a sombrero I could find was a Raiders of the Lost Ark hat, which Lisa decorated with Mexican accoutrements.

As usual, I set up shop at the end of the driveway. My taco stand was a work of art – three big, colorful signs and a table backed with sauces and oils and a taco oven. Sometimes, I'm overwhelmed by my own brilliance.

This time, despite the subzero temperatures, Lisa came out to see what I was doing. I'm pretty sure it was the first time she went out of her way to witness my inanity – and, no, that's not a typo; I didn't intend to write "insanity." A taco stand in the snow may be inane, but it's not insane.

Lisa posted a picture of it online to get a reaction from her friends, which is fine because it's different and different is good. People may love your selfies and motivational quotes – but, no, they don't.

When Mallory saw it on Facebook, she posted it on Reddit. She does that sometimes because she loves reading the comments about her father.

A couple hours later, Mallory called and said I was going viral.

"Dad, you're at the top of Reddit's Front Page."

"What does that mean?"

"You're the top ranking, number one!"

"Number one in what, Glens Falls?"

"Number one in the world!"

It wound up getting 110,000 "Upvotes," which attracted the attention of *BuzzFeed*, the *Albany Times Union* and several local and national TV stations. Mallory even got requests from a talk show in Texas and Fox News in Phoenix. She forwarded them to me, but I didn't return their messages.

I set up the taco stand to see what would happen. I got my answer. All that stuff in the last paragraph happened.... and it never stopped happening. That photo is being used for a million different things in a million different places. People are constantly forwarding me various sightings of it, like this one, from *Fatherly.com,* which ran this headline:

"THIS DAD DECIDED TO BE HIS WEIRDEST SELF DURING THE BOMB CYCLONE."

If they think that's my "weirdest self," it's because they've never heard me take a shower.

The reporters from *Buzzfeed* and the *Times Union* wanted to know more about my alcoholism. I'll never turn down a request to talk about that. If I can spare one family the agony of watching a loved one drink himself to death, I'll talk about my own experience all day.

About a month later, Glens Falls got pounded with twice as much snow. This time, I set up a long table with rolled up towels, lotions and oils, warm stones and potted plants for ambience.

That's right – Swedish Massage.

It was risky. With the lemonade and taco stands, I was trying to attract the attention of the plow drivers. This time, I tried blocking my signs every time the plows came by. I really didn't want to stand in the snow, running my fingers through the hairy back of some dude named Smitty.

Again, Lisa came out with her camera.

An hour later, a TV assignment editor called and asked if she could send a reporter and camera crew to the house. This time I said yes -- only because Lisa told me to. Besides, based on the amount of snow on our street, I was positive they'd never make it there. But they did, and I stood out there for a half hour in my tank top doing the interview.

A few neighbors stopped to see what was going on. I couldn't concentrate on the reporter's questions because I was wondering if these were the same neighbors who saw me in the middle of the woods on the riding mower a few months earlier.

I prayed it was because that is some funny shit. I could just hear them grumbling in their cars as they passed by.

Goddamn it! Our property value is going down!

The reporter must have seen one of the articles that mentioned my alcoholism. Or maybe she thought I was drunk. Either way, she wanted to talk about my drinking. I told her what I've been telling other people all along.

"Once you remove all that alcohol, you never know what was hiding underneath. I guess this is just the person I was supposed to be all along."

Her reaction – and, of course, reactions are what I live for -- was hilarious. She tilted her head slightly and looked down like she had something to say but wasn't sure how to say it.

"So, this is the person you..."

And then she just stopped.

"Yeah," I told her. "Take the alcohol out of this alcoholic, and this is what's behind Door Number Two – a Swedish massage stand in a snowbank."

I also told her, "This is my way of letting my kids know I'm okay now."

She didn't take the bait. I was hoping she'd say, "So this is how you tell your kids you're okay?"

The next day, an old guy I'd never seen came up to me in the gym.

"So, you're the massage man?"

I gave him a disgusted look.

"What do you mean?"

He thought he made a mistake and he froze. His face looked like it was ready for an autopsy.

The massage stand was a success. I scored another award-winning reaction, but it wasn't even on the same scale as the one I accidentally got out of Suzie one night.

I was sitting between her and Vick R. at an unusually large meeting in Hudson Falls one night. Due to extremely tragic circumstances, it was solemn meeting. We were discussing the difficult subject of family and addiction.

I've lost track of how young people have died from overdoses since I've been in the program – people I knew or whose parents I still know. On that night, we were mourning the loss of yet another one.

Obviously, it's a scary subject for me, given the gene I inherited and most likely passed on to Mallory and Jackson. All around me, kids their age are dropping dead from drugs. It only takes one time, one bad decision or one encounter with anything laced with fentanyl. In the rooms of AA, we are tragically reminded of it on a regular basis. It literally keeps me up at night.

None of that changes the fact that, when someone says a word that can even remotely be construed as sexual, I start giggling like a nine-year-old in sex education class. Certain words just do that do me. It's part of my disease – I just don't know which one.

Here's what happened. At the beginning of the meeting, someone was talking about the stiffness in her back. That's fine. I can ignore "stiffness." But then another person spoke, and even though they meant to say "shift," I heard "shaft."

I didn't laugh. I just looked down and scratched the back of my neck.

Unlike every other adult in the room, I had two things lingering in my head -- "stiffness" and "shaft" – two completely innocent words that my simple mind automatically interpreted as something perverted. That should have stopped happening when I turned twelve.

The next person was talking about the pure and harmless subject of praying, but then she got all dramatic about it.

"I knew what I needed, so I just dropped to my knees."

I looked around, waiting for everyone to bust out laughing. No one made a sound. I surveyed every face in the room. Not even a smile. Even the two other childish pigs in the room had straight faces.

What the fuck is wrong with these people? "She dropped to her knees!" I mean, come on! Why is no one laughing?

Miss Stiff, Mr. Shaft, and Mrs. knees – the three of them were dancing around like naked elves in my undeveloped brain. It was literally out of my control.

Trust me, I tried to hold it in. I knew it would be taboo to laugh at any point of the discussion. We laugh in meetings all the time, just not at *this* meeting. It was a sad subject. I was sad too.

Then, Dave, a friend of mine, started speaking. I was itching for him to say something funny, so I could pretend to be laughing at him while letting it all out.

Problem is, even when everyone is screwing around, Dave isn't very funny, and he was especially unfunny that night.

It was almost time for our 8:30 break. I just had to hold it together for another five minutes.

Just pay attention to Dave. It would be so fucked up if you laughed right now.

I lifted my extra-large Dunkin Donuts coffee from my knee, raised it to my mouth and took a big sip. That's when Dave delivered the deathblow. He said something about the importance of meetings and how he tries to come at least five times a week.

I had fought the good fight, but now it was over.

My hand, the one holding the cup, clenched. The cup, with its airtight cover, didn't just crumple; it exploded, sending coffee in three directions – down, forward and to the left, all over Suzie's shoulders and hair.

Then there was the coffee in my mouth. At first, it was well contained, streaming down my chin and onto my lap. That was before I saw the coffee in Suzie's hair, at which point it misted out between my lips until I gave up and just spit it out on the floor.

Is it possible my mind was subconsciously trolling for dirty words to avoid thinking about the sensitive subject being discussed? Maybe, but I think Dr. Stiller would have a different opinion. Try and follow this:

This disease is killing our young people, and communities are drenched in the poison that's doing it – alcohol, heroin, opioids, meth, crack, benzodiazepines. In the rooms, we experience the consequences more than anyone because we used them ourselves, and addiction is a family disease.

It's unbelievable how much square footage an extra-large cup of Dunkin Donuts coffee can cover. Then there was the splatter. That went even further.

Nothing scares me more than Mallory or Jackson thinking they can outsmart this disease. By the time they realize they can't -- that the disease is stronger than them -- just as it was stronger than me -- the disease will have them in its grip.

The coffee catastrophe created two kinds of splatter. The first was the splatter from the hand crunch and subsequent explosion. That's the splatter that took out Suzie. The other splatter, which went for twenty-seven miles, was caused when the primary mass of coffee hit the floor.

What destroys a lot of young lives is the fatal thinking that abusing alcohol is any less deadly than experimenting with drugs like heroin or meth. Abusing either will kill you; one just tends to take longer than the other. Most dead crack addicts got the courage to take their first hit when they were drunk.

It's amazing how many alcoholics it takes to clean up one coffee spill. I counted eleven – chair movers, paper towelers, moppers, grief counselors, all pitching together to get coffee off the floor and out of Suzie's hair.

The last several paragraphs are disarranged on purpose, as a demonstration of how my mind ticks and tocks, from good to bad, funny to sad, normal to fucked up. My brain needs constant supervision.

Which leads me back to Dr. Stiller.

For all the time I've spent speculating about why I overdosed in 2003, not once did I consider the obvious possibility: Maybe I'm crazy.

For all the time I spent wondering why I take so many medications, not once did I ask the doctor who prescribed them.

For all the time I spent in hospitals, rehabs and mental facilities, not once have I asked to see my medical files.

I must have been diagnosed by more than a dozen doctors, but I've never cared what other people think, and that includes doctors. It's not even that I would disagree with their diagnoses; I literally didn't care... until I *needed* to care, not for my sake, for Jackson's.

Here's where the book gets unfunny again.

Chapter Twenty-Four

Jackson's Hell

FOUR YEARS AND FOUR MONTHS SOBER

For most of 2016 and 2017, Jackson suffered in silence. It wasn't until the end of his senior year that his mother and I comprehended the severity of the condition he was trying to battle on his own.

Jackson was suffering from all the afflictions that led me to drink when I was his age, but his symptoms were a lot worse than mine ever were.

From the time he uttered his first words, Jackson was excited about every little thing. You could paint a rock and give it to him and he'd be grateful for a year.

By 2017, at seventeen, Jackson was no longer that kid. Over the course of about six months, he began slipping away, downward. He slowly became detached from the rest of the world, depressed and, at times, impossible to talk to, impossible to reason with and impossible to reach.

We had no idea what happened to our sweet, eager, happy kid. His mother was sending me messages saying he was constantly locked in his room. He was throwing up in the morning, complaining about his stomach and insisting he couldn't go to school.

Suddenly, the outgoing kid who was always in a good mood was too miserable to be around other people, even for a few minutes.

My heart breaks when I imagine my son locked in his room, researching his symptoms, trying desperately to figure out what was wrong with him. He studied everything he could find to understand his mood swings, depression, anxiety and even paranoia.

He scoured the internet for solutions -- supplements, herbal remedies, over-the-counter medicines. He asked his mother to take him to his family doctor, repeatedly, but he could never find the right way to explain what was happening to him, and he'd leave even more depressed than when he went in.

He was determined to figure it out on his own. As time went on, his condition worsened, to the point where he was in danger of not graduating high school. That's when he started to tell us more about what he was experiencing.

He began texting me when he was having severe episodes of confusion or distress. The texts scared me. My son was nowhere to be found in the words I was reading. The messages were irrational and paranoid.

Sometimes they were rants that I knew would make no sense to him the next day. Whatever was plaguing my son was beyond my comprehension.

His mother and I discussed the options. Selfishly, I hated all of them because I didn't want to admit that he wasn't going to just snap out of it.

I had already made one mistake several months earlier; I just didn't realize it at the time.

Jackson knew about my overdose in 2003 and my subsequent psychiatric stays. One night, out of the blue, he texted me, asking what they diagnosed me with.

In hindsight, my response could have been... my response sucked.

"To tell you the truth, I don't even know, and I never bothered to ask."

Both things are true. I knew I'd been diagnosed with something, but I didn't bother to get the details. Problem was, he wasn't just asking because he was curious; he was asking because he wanted to know what he inherited.

He dropped the subject quickly the first time but asked again a few weeks later. This time, I realized why he was asking, but got the sense he was worried about the stigma.

He'd spent a lot of time researching and now he had pinpointed what might be wrong with him.

At first, I downplayed the results of his research. Even though he'd always been an excellent student, his condition was keeping him out of school so often that he was in danger of not graduating. I was worried that he was going to self-prophesize his way further downward.

All of this was happening to Jackson a lot earlier in life than it happened to me. I thought he could fight his way through it, just for a few more months, until after graduation.

I thought he could ride it out for a little while like I did... except I *didn't*. I never willed it away or ignored it or used mind control to weather the storm. I drank it away.

In the end, he found the strength to do all those things, clawing his way through classes and graduating – by a mile – with the rest of his class in the Spring of 2017.

Which leads me back to Chris Cornell whose talents Jackson admired and whose struggles as a teen were very much like Jackson's.

In May of 2017, when Jackson was suffering the most, Cornell hung himself after a performance -- for no reason that was apparent to anyone around him.

That night, Jackson sent me a series of texts, agonizing over Cornell's shocking suicide.

"I'm really struggling with this."

I called his mother and she went to his room and talked with him about it until we were both thoroughly convinced that he was sad, not suicidal.

I'd gone from hoping Jackson would be the next Chris Cornell to fearing he might be. Cornell was in his fifties. I couldn't stop agonizing over the prospect of Jackson struggling with this disease for the rest of his life.

I MADE MISTAKES WITH Jackson's situation. In the hour of decision, it took me way too long to recognize what was happening. Still, there was a reason I pushed Jackson to finish the school year before getting treatment. I knew treating him was going to be a process, not just a visit to the doctor's office.

I've never been able to brook the thought of Jackson inheriting any facet of my past. For that reason, I was reluctant to bring him to Stiller, but it was a selfish reluctance.

Sure, there were plenty of other psychiatrists out there. But, with my treatment records, Stiller would be able to pinpoint and treat Jackson's condition a lot quicker than any other doctor could.

Today, Jackson is under the care of Dr. Stiller. For the first few visits, his mother and I sat in on his appointments. I continue to go because my history is relevant to his treatment. In fact, whenever Jackson has an appointment, Dr. Stiller pulls both of our files.

For Jackson's sake, I force myself to take an interest in my own diagnosis. I don't understand my insouciance, but it's still there today.

Jackson and I are very much alike. Perhaps if I had been more like Jackson – if I had been more curious about my condition thirty years ago -- I could have saved myself a lot of trouble, not to mention beer money, interaction with police, overdoses, rehabs, hospital visits and court dates.

Jackson was going to need medications – probably for the rest of his life. Stiller began the trial and error process of pinpointing what medications were going to help him.

Me not giving a shit was never a good enough reason to boycott the truth. It was time to educate myself. I started by researching my own prescriptions. I knew that would help Stiller's diagnostic process. Obviously, he already knows what he's prescribing me, but only I remember how we got there.

I Googled my medications. According to everything I found, they were anti-seizure meds.

That made no sense. I've never had seizure. Some alcoholics have seizures when they first stop drinking, but those are an early withdrawal effect. There's was no reason for me to be taking them four years after my last drink.

By the way, I get that I was doing this the hard way. I get that all the research and guesswork was totally unnecessary. I get that I could have just picked up the phone, called Stiller and asked him what he was treating me for. I get all of that.

But if I had done it that way, he'd have given me a definitive answer. I didn't want that. I wanted options. I didn't want the undisputed truth. I wanted several answers to choose from so I could pick the one that I was most comfortable with.

That's how it always works when you Google something medical. You never get one answer; you get a handful of answers that seem plausible.

That didn't happen this time.

The psych and seizure meds I was on were anti-psychotic drugs. Obviously, I knew I was taking four different medications, but I thought they were for post-alcohol... whatever.

The meds aren't mind-altering drugs designed to give me a buzz or put me in a good mood. They just make me feel normal. You'll notice I said *feel*, not *act*. No one describes me that way – and, just like it is with everything else, I don't want to know.

It's most accurate to say that that the meds make me act and behave the way I was born to behave, without the chemicals in my brain being sprayed around my head like they were shooting from a lawn sprinkler.

Not unexpectedly, Jackson, my genetic progeny, wound up needing the same medication as me – an anti-seizure med that keeps the angry neon butterflies away.

The change in him was more dramatic than it was when I started taking medication. It was like someone reached under his shirt and flipped a switch.

The whole episode was surreal. It was as if Jackson had been kidnapped by a disorder that turned him into a son I never knew. Then, in just a matter of days, the medicine brought him back to me. He came back, not as the way he was a year or even two years ago, but the way he was as a boy – eager, happy-go-lucky and carefree -- before the disorder snatched him away.

Jackson was going to be okay. In a way, he was going to be better than okay. My biggest fear, from the time he was born, was that he would succumb to genetic, alcoholic tendencies. Maybe these medications would subvert those tendencies.

I'm going to make sure it turns out that way. For the balance of my weird existence, that is the one thing I'll treat with unwavering seriousness.

When Jackson started playing guitar as a boy, I not only encouraged him, I did everything I could to stimulate his talent. A lot of other parents will do the same thing, but only with the caveat, "Just as long as you realize it'll never be a career." Fuck that. If he can turn his guitar into a career, I'll be prouder of him than if he was a U.S. Senator – a lot prouder. Make that a million times prouder.

Jackson is sicker than I was at his age, but he's more responsible, more mature and less odd. If the medications continue to work, he'll be the person he was meant to be. Every day, I grow more excited to see that future unfold.

Chapter Twenty-Five

Didn't God Make Lamotrigine?

SOBER AND BETTER THAN EVER

A funny thing occurred to me while I was researching medications. My incredible day of clarity at Crandall Park in 2014 *was*, in fact, a miracle – kind of.

I was reading about the medicines I was taking -- their symptoms, side effects, absorption rates -- and I cross-referenced all that information with a few other factors, including a calendar.

My day at Crandall Park – my miraculous day of clarity -- wasn't just the fog of alcohol lifting. That may have been *part* of it, but mostly it was the effects of Lamotrigine and the rest of my psych meds kicking in.

There are miracles and then there are *miracles*. There are miracles of God, miracles of science, miracles of nature and Miracles on Ice. There's even a Miracle Ear. For some of us, there's a miracle drug. It's just a matter of, well, miracles – and perspective.

The question is: What came first, the clarity or the Lamotrigine? In my case, it was the truth.

My diagnosis was always at my fingertips; it was just a matter of me having the courage to look at it. Once I did, I saw what Stiller had been jotting down in his notepad for all these years.

I never would have coined the term "mood spike" if I'd known there was already a name for it. Again, it's a mere matter of perspective... and semantics. I say tomato, doctors say bipolar.

I saw this coming for at least a decade. In my last book, I alluded to the possibility that, sooner or later, I would get diagnosed with something weird.

I also quoted a song my grandmother used to sing to me: *Que Sera, Sera.* It's Spanish for "who gives a shit," although that's more of an interpretation than a direct translation.

If it didn't affect Jackson – and, aside from having to take medication, I pray it won't – I wouldn't care at all.

If anything, getting a diagnosis was a good thing -- for me and for Jackson. Now, he won't have to wonder what's going in his head in the future, and I won't have to wonder what was going on in my head in the past.

Specifically, I won't have to wonder why I did so many almost-unforgiveable things when I *wasn't* drinking, things I always attributed to alcohol withdrawal.

All these years, Stiller was the only one who knew what I meant by "mood spikes," but he couldn't help me until I quit drinking... and that wasn't gonna happen.

So, I treated it myself. When I felt mood spikes (I'm still going to call them that) I'd start drinking, no matter where I was. If I was already drinking, I'd adjust my meds... meaning, I'd drink faster.

Alcohol, as deadly as it is for me, was good for one thing: It always stopped the mood spikes. I need to not remember that.

There were a few times when I couldn't drink fast enough to outrun a mood spike. Two times, the results were disastrous.

The first time – the worst one – led to the Klonopin overdose in 2003. I almost died that time, but Vick R. says there are worse things than death. For ten years after the overdose, I proved it.

The second disaster was in 2008. It started when I was wandering around Lake George by myself one night. I was having trouble drinking fast enough to quash the mood spikes. In the process of trying, I got thrown out of a bar.

On the way to the next bar, I called Dr. Stiller's office and left a hysterical voicemail.

It was one of those rare moments when I was lucid enough to know something wasn't right and honest enough to say it out loud – very loud. I was standing in the middle of a crowded sidewalk, screaming the same thing over and over into the phone

"No matter how much I drink, it won't go away."

By the time Stiller called back, I was already drunk and "cured." What followed was two weeks of rampant violence. It started with an attack on Mallory's bus driver.

The following day, I attacked on my ex-wife's lawyer in open court, broke a restraining order against her boyfriend and unleashed a full-out assault on Big Eminem.

I was convinced – the way a neurotic person *would* be – that Stiller would use the voicemail to put me away. For an entire year, I dodged his calls and blew off my appointments.

I drank harder than ever for the next five years and didn't have symptoms again until I got out of rehab in 2013 and moved in with Lisa. Lucky girl.

She knew I was bipolar, and she put up with my unpredictability for nine months. That's when the Lamotrigine kicked in at Crandall Park and everyone lived happily after ever.

The fact that the Lamotrigine worked confirmed Stiller's diagnosis. *Que sera, sera.*

There's a bright side to everything, and even when there's not, a crazy alcoholic can invent one.

The alcoholic side of my brain is always sending me messages:

If a little Lamotrigine is good, a lot of Lamotrigine must be great. Better yet, if I want to get a little crazy, I can just take no Lamotrigine.

Seriously, for about thirty seconds, that seemed like a good idea. I even thought of a logical reason to do it.

Remember that stack of op-eds I found, the ones I wrote in record-breaking time back in 2010? I never understood why I wrote them or how I managed to write so many so fast. Then I realized, I was probably in the throes of a manic upswing.

Not too long ago, the alcoholic side of my brain floated this brilliant idea:

Let's skip the Lamotrigine for a few days to expedite the writing of this book.

What stopped me? Two things.

1) The *other* side of my brain -- the one that's been going to AA for more than four years – saw my mania taking a wrong turn. It envisioned me wearing Lisa's wedding dress while painting the driveway orange with Bam's tail.

At that point, the neighbors would just take up a pool to hire a hit man.

2) I never really considered it. It was just another sick thought that only an alcoholic mind could conceive – and I'll be listening to him and his crazy cousin, Spike Moody, for the rest of my life.

I'VE HEARD PEOPLE in AA talk about the "gift of alcoholism" and express gratitude for being born an alcoholic.

"Otherwise," they say. "We wouldn't know the glory of recovery."

I don't know about all *that.* Personally, I'd rather know the glory of recovery without having to inaugurate it with the agony of addiction.

Better yet, it would be nice to know the glory of having two beers with the guys instead of thirty-six by myself. And I would gladly surrender the glory of recovery to give my kids the glory of a life without it.

For me, being an alcoholic entailed using one deadly disease to cover up another. When I was drunk, I was a danger to myself. When I was sober and unmedicated, I was a danger to everyone.

I don't know if death is funny. I know my next one will be. It's gotta be funnier than the last one. I can guarantee one thing: Everything leading up to it is going to be both funny and recorded.

If I wind up in a nursing home, I'll be the one recording the other patients' faces while I eat chocolate pudding out of a bedpan.

I'll be the one smearing Vaseline on the handles of everyone's walkers.

After my sponge baths, I'll ask for a happy ending.

If the nurses abuse me, I'll pretend to enjoy it and ask for more.

My friends in AA talk about the honor of dying sober. Yeah, I can't wait.

Is there a medal for honor on the other side of this life? If there is, I'll trade mine for a bowl of Oxycontin.

Are you listening Lisa, Mallory and Jackson? If I have so much as a headache, load me up. Bring on the morphine and barbiturates and whatever else they've got in the candy closet. Go to the corner and get me Molly, and I'm not talking about our dog Molly.

Grab me some Christy, some Moon Gas, some Poppers and a little Lucy – and maybe even a tablespoon of Wack. Let me take a victory lap, high as a tetradactyl on ecstasy.

And when that's all done, don't forget to buy a black Sharpie for my wake. Write dirty, humiliating stuff all over my dead face. Then record people's reactions when they walk up to kneel. That'll go down as the funniest thing I ever pulled off. And, yeah, I'm taking the credit. It doesn't matter who does it. It was my idea.

I don't have to look for a bright side anymore. These days, all sides are bright. My family and friends are safe and happy. They're right where they want to be, or going there, and I have my Great Purpose. It's to keep them guessing and laughing.

If I'm not laughing at something -- just because it's not funny -- I'm not looking at it from the right angle.

NEW YORK STATE GOVERNMENT is rarely a source of wisdom, but there's one thing it does (probably by accident) that makes a ton of sense.

It has to do with the State retirement package I'll collect in a few years. It's not based on my average salary over the course of my fifteen years in the State Retirement Fund. It's based on the years I shined, my three highest years.

That's the only equitable way to do it. If they did it any other way, I'd be punished for my early years with Monroe County and my part-time job with the Town of Chester. In other words, my low years would bring me down.

The irony is that my three best years as a salary-earner were my three worst years as an alcoholic. Being drunk was more profitable than being sober.

Which is better?

I've thought about this. What's the point of shining at all? In the long run, does it even matter?

Why should we waste time being good when being bad feels so much better? Why be honest if dishonest is easier? Why eat healthy if unhealthy tastes better? Why have sex with your own spouse when your neighbor's spouse is sexier?

Am I living the way I want to shine? Do I really want to be a shimmering taco stand in the snow?

Given what I've publicly revealed about my alcoholism and, now, mental health, do I really want to be seen in a tank top doing Swedish massages and psychic readings at the end of the driveway in February?

Is that how I want to be seen? Aren't I going out of my way to denigrate myself, fulfilling my own negative stereotype?

Is that what I want on the front and back cover of my book? Does that guy look like he can even spell his name?

Yes and no, respectively. Yes, it's what I want on the cover because I couldn't think of anything else. And no, he doesn't look like he can spell his name.

Sure, I could have used a picture of me in a suit, reviewing speeches from fifteen years ago when I was better dressed and better looking -- but that's when I was drunk and unstable.

At the end of the day, I take a good look around me, just to see who's still listening and laughing. It's always the people I wanted to be there in the first place. It's always the people whose smile I want to shine the brightest.

Life isn't all strawberries and sunsets.

I still get haunted by things that never happened. Juan is still complaining about you-know-who. Jackson is still adjusting. Mom is still ignoring all things fatal. Mallory is still ignoring the eye rollers. And Lisa is still trying to sleep through my late-night yodeling.

Courtney has been drunk several times since detox. Connor is struggling. Another friend just relapsed for the third time in two years. The miracle is that they keep coming back.

Boon and Andy are still gone.

The miracle is that they left their two-foot square signed with their honor – and, here we are, still thinking about them.

One week before this book went to print, Dr. Stiller suffered a major stroke, ending his four-decade medical practice. The miracle is that he lived, and we all press on.

Juan left a holy mess in Springfield. I left a mess there and everywhere else.

This spring, he'll have seven years sober. I'll be chairing his celebration. The miracle is that our three best years are in the future, not the past -- and the best part is, we know it.

The miracle isn't that we survived. The miracle is that we're living, that it's never too late to shine. The miracle is that we're beating the drum and getting even with our past.

All this other stuff -- the lemonade and the sharpies -- are just things to laugh about on the way there -- things I thought up in the shower, where only one opinion matters.

That's where I have my best ideas. I never second-guess anything my brain dreams up in there. I never overrule myself. I just dry off fast and walk in the direction of my dream.

Sometimes I stumble, but I never change my mind, and it feels good to be that free.

THE END

Afterword

"Fuck you, faggot!"

(The children of Hudson Falls are so charming... and clever)

That's all I heard as I whizzed by in my tinker toy of an automobile. My Kia Soul, which looks like a white Lego with wheels, begs for that sort of abuse. You can scream anything you want at a Soul. What's the driver going to do, beat you with his scarf?

If that had been me five years ago, it would have gone down a different way. For starters, since I was behind the wheel of a car, I would have been reasonably sober.

After getting a DWAI in 2011, I never drove with alcohol in my system again, which means I hardly ever drove. And because I would have been sober five years ago, I'd have also been angry and ready to fight at the slightest provocation.

Just ask Big Eminem, the guy I chased down and nearly killed in 2012 after he flashed me his little "gang signs." To this day, that guy must be wondering where he went wrong. "What, you can't hang with the boys and trash talk passing cars?"

Of course, Big Eminem didn't even say anything; he was just trying to impress his black friends by dissing the man. They most likely weren't impressed watching me use his head like a gavel, banging it repeatedly against, of all things, a speed bump.

I never said anything either. I'm sure the first thing onlookers always told the police was, "He didn't say a

308

word. He just ran over and started punching. It was so weird."

It's not that weird. If I ran up and did that, the guy had to be begging for it. And why would I say anything? What should I be saying, the "Pledge of Allegiance?" Now that would be funny. I'm suddenly mad at myself for not thinking of it ten years ago.

Police: "What set him off?"

Witness: "I don't know, he just started swinging while saying the Pledge of Allegiance."

To this day, Big Eminem must be wondering, "What in the hell did I do to deserve that?" Sometimes, just being an asshole is enough. Other times, crossing paths with an alcoholic who needs a drink is enough. Doing both at the same time is always enough.

If you're not crazy, you must be crazy. Think about it. We're put here for a very short time and we're told to make the best of our lives before they're over.

So, why should we waste time being good when being bad feels so much better? Why be honest if dishonest is easier? Why eat healthy if unhealthy tastes better? Why go to church on Sunday if the pregame show is more entertaining? Why have sex with your own spouse when your neighbor's spouse is sexier?

And, why in God's name would anyone run ten miles every morning when staying home and eating bacon feels and tastes so much better? Runner's high, really? It's more like "runner's myocardial infarction." Triathletes have been dropping faster than microdots at a Dead show.

If you can't answer these questions, the uncertainties of life have probably driven you crazy. If you can answer these questions, the uncertainties of life have definitely driven you crazy.

No?

Come with me to Stiller's office. Let's see how you make out.

BACK IN HUDSON FALLS, me and my one-cylinder hamster-mobile turned the other cheek and kept buzzing along. The "pedestrian" who called me a faggot was still freaking out in the background.

The new me would pray for him. I couldn't even write that with a straight face.

The church I was headed to was just up the road. As soon as I got there, they asked me to chair the meeting. You're supposed to never say no, and why would I?

It was the perfect opportunity to brag about my restraint a mile back.

"It was serenity in the face of aggression," I told them

For the rest of the night, nothing happened. The police weren't looking for me. I didn't have to drench my knuckles in hydrogen peroxide. No one was mad at me.

On the way home, I stopped at Cumberland Farms and got two boxes of Nature Valley Fruit and Nut granola bars.

Bam and Lisa were waiting for me when I walked in the door. I kissed one of them on the head and other one on the lips, and Lisa said, "Don't kiss me on the head like I'm a dog."

I'm not the guy I was in the last book, which is the only reason I'm alive to write another one. By the way, the original title of this book was, "The Crazy Thing About Being Sober."

I changed it for obvious reasons. Why give away the ending on the front cover?

About the Author

JOHN C. WOLFE IS THE AUTHOR of "You Can't Die: A Day of Clarity." He is the former Chief Speechwriter to New York Governor George E. Pataki. He has worked as an advertising copywriter, a magazine editor and a Senior Writer for two County Executives in Rochester and the SUNY Chancellor's Office in Albany. He was Pataki's Chief Speechwriter for nearly ten years. In 2007, he abandoned his writing career, retreated to the Adirondacks and worked as a Zoning Officer in Chestertown, New York. His writing was limited to a series of published op-eds in several newspapers, including the New York Times and the Times of Israel. He began writing about his drinking experience in 2015 and completed "You Can't Die: A Day of Clarity" in 2016.

You Can't Die

A Day of Clarity

JOHN C. WOLFE

AMAZON   KINDLE   GOOGLE BOOKS

Five Stars on

Amazon and Kindle

You Can't Die: A Day of Clarity

From Amazon and Kindle readers

49 total Reviews

48 five stars ☆☆☆☆☆

1 four stars ☆☆☆☆

98 percent overall rating

"Beautifully written, poignant memoir by one of the most gifted writers today." *~Karen Lehrman Bloch, Author of "Passage to Israel" and "The Inspired Home"*

THIS BOOK IS A RAW, real look into not only the world of an alcoholic but into a little thought about part of the political world, a speechwriter. His personal and professional life laid completely open for the reader was sometimes sad, sometimes intriguing and always spellbinding. His personal, firsthand experience of 9/11 as the Chief Speechwriter for the governor of New York created a whole other perspective of that day and the aftermath for me. I couldn't put A Day of Clarity down and in the end wanted to know more about this man and his life. My hope is to hear much more from John C. Wolfe soon. ✰✰✰✰✰ *on Amazon/Kindle*

THIS IS WRITTEN with great candor and humor. John's story engages the reader very early on and highlights his challenges with alcohol as well as his behavior issues while trying to achieve sobriety. The intensity and duration of his disease makes me wonder how he was physically able to survive. ✰✰✰✰✰ *on Amazon/Kindle*

I FOUND "YOU CAN'T DIE: A Day of Clarity" to be an extraordinary and completely engaging read. It is a very honest and painful look into the powerful and enslaving world of alcoholism and Wolfe's personal life struggles. The chapters are skillfully woven together with intense human drama, raw and naked emotion and much humor: such as when Wolfe describes how he would often, late at night, walk around inside the Albany state capital building in his underwear. It is an absolute miracle that Wolfe is here today to tell this story. We can thank his incredibly loyal and loving family and friends and ultimately Wolfe's willingness to see the value in living life without alcohol. ✰✰✰✰ *on Amazon/Kindle*

BRILLIANT AND well written, couldn't put it down.
✰✰✰✰✰ *on Amazon/Kindle*

EXCEEDINGLY PERSONAL ACCOUNT of the author's private battle with booze. I can only imagine the courage it took to write his story. ✫✫✫✫✫ *on Amazon/Kindle*

"NOT TYPICALLY A READER of this sort of book, I saw a post by the author's daughter on Reddit.com -- a post that had nothing to do with promoting the book but rather showing a photo of a quirky and funny Christmas tradition her father has. Upon reading the comments, I began to learn about some of the struggles that the author has faced in life and wondered "how did he get from there to where he is in this photo?" It wasn't easy, for sure. I recommend this book to anybody who enjoys a good, entertaining writing style and interesting story. The writing is brutally honest, witty, heartfelt and at times very funny. Almost like a funny joke at a funeral at which you just can't help chuckling." ✫✫✫✫✫ *on Amazon/Kindle*

WOLFE WRITES ABOUT his struggle with alcoholism with a raw authenticity rarely found in a memoir. I read it in one sitting, quite literally unable to put it down. He shows how alcohol can hold someone in its grip and make it impossible to function without it. His talent as a writer is on full display as he tells his shocking story with sincerity, humor, and tenderness. ✫✫✫✫✫ *on Amazon/Kindle*

"WOLFE WRITES WITH A profound sophistication, while still maintaining an effortless nature that makes this quite the page turner. Years as a speech writer have undoubtedly taught him to make a narrative that is clear, concise, eloquent, and thematic, while still being an absolute joy to take in. This book is a story of redemption, love, loss, and rebranding that is simply impossible to put down. To read it is to learn from it, and I'm a better person now than I was before I read it." ✫✫✫✫✫ *on Amazon/Kindle*

THIS WAS A TERRIFIC READ! A very emotional story that many can relate to. Great job by the author making you feel if you were right there with him. Highly recommend. ✫✫✫✫✫ *Melanie Sarafin, Amazon/Kindle*

"GRITTY, DARK, AND PROVOCATIVE. Autobiography, political intrigue, insider disclosures, self-help, I'm not sure which label fits, but the one that matters most is brilliant." ✫✫✫✫✫ *Joshua B. Toas on Amazon/Kindle*

IT TOOK A LOT OF COURAGE to share this story. It's a captivating look at addiction from the inside looking out-a view so well described that I felt as though I was there with him. This is a great book for an addict, anyone in recovery and especially for those who love an addict. Thank you for exposing the truth about addiction- your story will surely help others. ✰✰✰✰✰ *on Amazon/Kindle*

WOLFE HAS A WAY of sharing his story so that it makes it seem as if you are either standing next to him the whole time or peering into a mirror at yourself. We all grapple with demons of our own and every one of us can relate to the choices that led John down a dangerous path. It could have gone so very wrong, but he decided to change. Then he did. His struggle is the human struggle. His success should be held up as a shining example. ✰✰✰✰✰ *Andie on Amazon/Kindle*

REFRESHINGLY HONEST and profound. Couldn't put it down. I found myself feeling a part of his journey. Compelling and real. ✰✰✰✰✰ *Sasha Radkova on Amazon/Kindle*

VERY WELL WRITTEN and engaging. A story that is difficult to forget, it is both humorous and somber and delivered with such authenticity, it will without a doubt help many, many others who are struggling with addiction. ✰✰✰✰ *on Amazon/Kindle*

EXCELLENT, INSPIRATIONAL, EDUCATIONAL. This book took a lot of brave honesty and thoughtfulness to write. It would be a great read for addicts and a wonderful teaching tool in rehab programs. I would recommend it to everyone who is dealing with addiction. Many of my friends read it and were very impressed with this author. ✰✰✰✰✰ *on Amazon/Kindle*

"EXCELLENT READ. The author takes you through an amazing personal journey of his life that is filled with laughter, heart break, friendships and family. A tough read at times and emotional but so well written. I highly recommend this book!" ✰✰✰✰✰ *Ken Rubenson on Amazon/Kindle*

"A BEAUTIFULLY WRITTEN MEMOIR. This book is a wonderful self-examination and reflection of one man's decades long struggle with alcoholism. The author's ability to write such a detailed and honest portrait of himself (the good, the bad and the ugly) was truly remarkable. His sarcasm, wit and sense of humor made reading about such a tough subject matter almost humorous at times. Throughout the book, you will truly root for this man to conquer his demons. Once I started, I could not put it down until I turned the final page." ✫✫✫✫✫ *Meg D. on Amazon/Kindle*

"MOVING AND DEEPLY Personal. Wolfe's story is a Beacon hope for those who are struggling to find their way to recovery."
✫✫✫✫ *on Amazon/Kindle*

"COULDN'T PUT THIS BOOK DOWN. From the start, you get hooked."
✫✫✫✫✫ *Jill Collinson on Amazon/Kindle*

"RAW, REAL, EMOTIONAL, funny and very well written."
✫✫✫✫✫ *on Amazon/Kindle*

"PAINFULLY RAW MEMOIR... relatable on so many levels. You will not be able to put this book down. Evokes every emotion - you will laugh and cry at the same time. Brave exposition and depiction of the impact addiction has on the sufferer and those who love them. Wish I could write a review that does the book justice. So proud for this author and the bravery and authenticity required to share his story." ✫✫✫✫✫ *Tara Scully on Amazon/Kindle*

"THROUGH WOLFE'S JOURNEY of personal survivorship, he informs us of things such as why the Baseball Hall of Fame's catalog was so much wordier in 1991 than it was in previous editions, through what it takes to sneak the beer a drinker needs to work in 9.11-era Manhattan, even on one's way to Ground Zero as a state government official, quick tips on how to deal with abusive school bus drivers and ignorant principals, and so much more... and then all it takes to get healthy and right again." ✫✫✫✫✫ *Jason Paluch on Amazon/Kindle*

"YOU WON'T WANT TO PUT IT DOWN. It almost feels wrong reading about the dirty secrets of someone of this caliber. You'll be happy he is still alive to write this story." ✫✫✫✫✫ *on Amazon/Kindle*

"**AN EXTREMELY RIVETING** and powerful book to read. Wolfe writes with such honesty that it makes this book sometimes difficult to read as he takes you through his pain and suffering with his struggles with addiction. But his style of writing, humor and personal accounts make this a book you are unable to put down until you reach the end." ☆☆☆☆☆ *Laurie on Amazon/Kindle*

"**THIS BOOK WAS A ROLLER COASTER** of emotions for me, one minute I was laughing out loud and the next my eyes would fill with tears. This book was written in a way, that kept me turning the page, I wanted to see what his next move would be. I hope, he will share more stories in the future, his Witt and gift for writing, had me not wanting the book to end." ☆☆☆☆☆
Katrina on Amazon/Kindle

PAINFULLY PERSONAL LIFE ASSESSMENT written in a brilliantly sarcastic manner that will make you wince, snort with laughter and wonder how it all came to be. A cautionary tale of epic proportions. His life's journey has been a twisted ride that you can't completely imagine, conveyed crisply by the man who by all accounts shouldn't have lived to tell his story. You will demand that your friends and family read this book. ☆☆☆☆☆ *on Amazon/Kindle*

"**WOLFE BRINGS US ALONG** on his wild ride with a writing style that will keep you riveted and eager for the next chapter. You won't want to put this down until you finish." ☆☆☆☆☆ *Louis A. Koehler on Amazon/Kindle*

Made in the USA
Columbia, SC
18 June 2024

37260121R00174